CW00651843

MOUNTAIN ASH TO NEATH

Vic Mitchell and Keith Smith

Cover picture: Weeds are growing on the platform of the highest station on the route, Hirwaun, as class 4300 2-6-0 no. 7310 heads east with a coal train in the twilight days of steam. (W.A.Camwell/SLS)

Published June 2006

ISBN 1 904474 80 2

Design Deborah Esher
Typesetting Barbara Mitchell

Published by
Middleton Press
Easebourne Lane
Midhurst, West Sussex
GU29 9AZ
Tel: 01730 813169
Fax: 01730 812601
Email: info@middletonpress.co.uk
www.middletonpress.co.uk

Printed & bound by Biddles Ltd, Kings Lynn

INDEX

ACKNOWLEDGEMENTS

We are very grateful for the assistance received from many of those mentioned in the credits also to A.R.Carder, R.S.Carpenter, L.Crosier, G.Croughton, N.Langridge, B.Lewis, Mr D. and Dr S.Salter and particularly our ever supportive wives, Barbara Mitchell and Janet Smith. Photographs attributed to RCT Libraries are reproduced by permission of Rhondda Cynon Taf Libraries and we are grateful to Mr N.Kelland for his assistance.

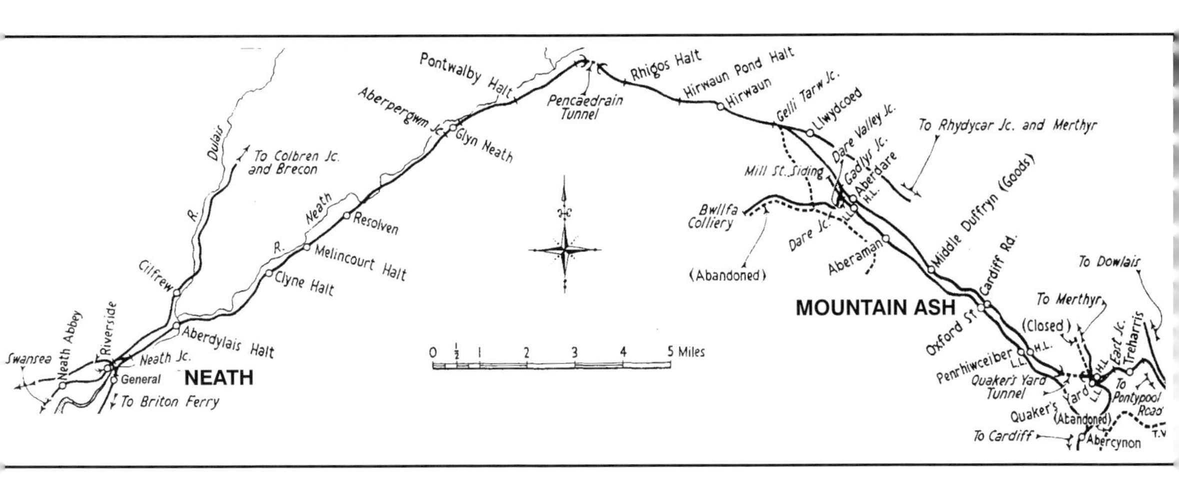

I. Plan of the route in 1955. (Railway Magazine)

GEOGRAPHICAL SETTING

The route is mostly over Coal Measures and climbs steadily from Mountain Ash to Hirwaun Pond. The Merthyr branch is in a tunnel for 1½ of its 7½ mile length, its eastern end falling at 1 in 100 in the tunnel and mostly at 1 in 51 to Merthyr station.

Mines were numerous in the Aberdare area, but most coal is now produced near Hirwaun and Glyn Neath, although there is now no track between these places. The latter is in the Vale of Neath, down which the line makes a steady descent for about ten miles to Neath.

There was once a port of note here, but it has for long been eclipsed by Swansea. The entire route was in Glamorganshire, except for 1½ miles near Hirwaun, which was in Brecknockshire.

All maps are at 15ins to 1 mile, with north at the top unless otherwise indicated.

II. Pre-1923 gradient profile.

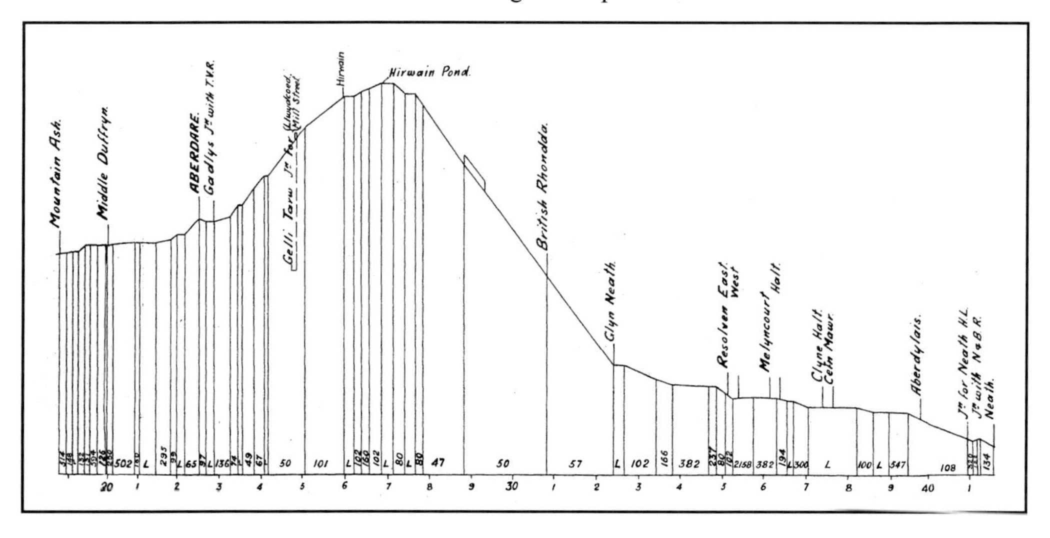

HISTORICAL BACKGROUND

The Vale of Neath Railway Act was passed on 3rd August 1846 and the route between Aberdare and Neath came into use on 24th September 1851. Although Merthyr was the prime objective, this line was delayed until 2nd November 1853, owing to the tunnel construction, and it effectively became a branch. I.K.Brunel was the engineer. The line was extended east to the Aberdare Canal in 1853 by the Aberdare Valley Railway. It reached Middle Duffryn in 1856 and was controlled by the VoNR from 1864.

The Great Western Railway acquired the VoNR in 1865, having taken over the South Wales Railway along the coast through Neath in 1863.

It fell to the GWR to close the gap and the section through Mountain Ash and Middle Duffryn was opened to passengers on 5th October 1864, this allowing through running between Hereford and Swansea. However, most of the traffic ran over only short lengths of the route and was mainly mineral, notably coal.

The VoNR and some tracks east of Aberdare were of broad gauge initially and of mixed gauge from 1863 until 1872, standard gauge prevailing thereafter in South Wales.

The GWR became the Western Region of British Railways upon nationalisation in 1948.

The line between Gelli Tarw Junction and Merthyr closed to all traffic on 31st December 1962 and passenger service between Pontypool Road and Neath via Mountain Ash was withdrawn on 11th June 1964.

The summit section between Hirwaun and Glyn Neath closed completely on 2nd October 1967, the lines each side remaining in use for mineral movements, mainly coal. Traffic was intermittent following the coal strikes of 1984-85, but the line reopened for regular traffic between Neath and Glyn Neath (Cwmgwrach) in March 1994. Aberdare to Hirwaun followed in January 1998, although the section had not closed completely.

The route between Mountain Ash and Aberdare reopened to passengers on 3rd October 1988, the trains from Cardiff using the 1846 ex-Taff Vale Railway lines for all but their final mile or so.

PASSENGER SERVICES

The initial service between Aberdare and Neath was of three weekday and two Sunday trains. The same frequency applied following the opening of the Merthyr line in 1853, but Aberdare was served by branch trains until through services began.

Following completion of the Middle Duffryn link in 1865, the GWR provided three through trains daily between Hereford and Swansea. A similar frequency was maintained over the route covered by this album for most of the 19th century, although there were only two Sunday trains for most of that period; there were fewer after World War I.

For most of the 20th century, there were five to seven trains between Pontypool Road and Neath, with two continuing direct to Swansea in the early years.

There continued to be one or two through trains between Merthyr and Neath (or Swansea) into the 20th century, but the branch itself had a greater frequency, up to ten trains each weekday.

There was an additional train between Aberdare and Neath (sometimes three) in most years from the 1920s to the end. There were also some to Swansea in the final years, these reversing at Neath General, but until 1936 there was a railmotor service direct to Swansea East Dock. Introduced in 1905, there were initially five weekday trips, all starting at Glyn Neath. The starting point for most journeys was Aberdare from 1912.

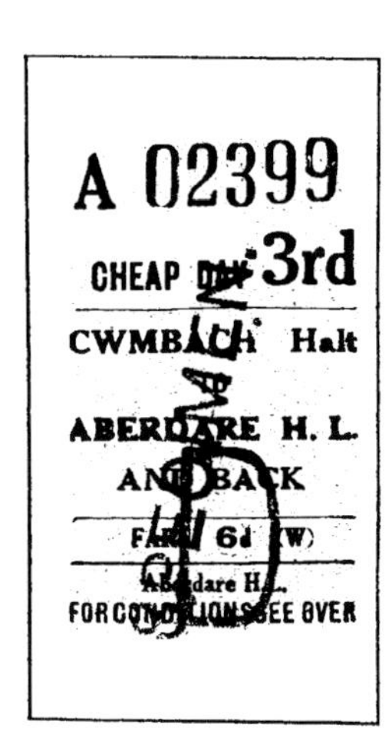

ABERDARE, MERTHYR, HIRWAIN, and NEATH.—Vale of Neath.

Miles	Fares 1st class	2nd class	3rd class	Down.	Wk Days 1 2 3 class	1 2 3 class	1 2 3 class	Sun. 1 2 3 class	1 2 3 class
	s. d.	s. d.	s. d.		mrn	aft	aft	mrn	aft
—	...	...	...	**Aberdare** ......dep	8 30	1 55	5 55	9 10	6 30
—	...	...	...	**Merthyr*** ... „	7 30	1255	4 55	8 10	5 30
2¼	0 6	0 4	0 2	Merthyr Road	8 41	2 6	6 6	9 21	6 41
3½	0 8	0 6	0 3	**Hirwain**	8 46	2 11	6 11	9 26	6 46
10	2 0	1 4	0 9	Glyn-Neath	9 7	2 32	6 32	9 49	7 7
12¾	2 8	1 8	1 0	Resolven	9 16	2 41	6 41	9 58	7 16
17¼	3 6	2 2	1 5	Aberdylais	9 25	2 50	6 50	10 8	7 25
19	3 8	2 4	1 7	**Neath** ....arr	9 30	2 55	6 55	1013	7 30
56¼	12 5	7 10	4 8	Carmarthen arr	1157	4 45	9 15	1220	9 40

Up.	Wk Days 1 2 3 class	1 2 3 class	1 2 3 class	Sun. 1 2 3 class	1 2 3 class
	mrn	mrn	aft	mrn	aft
Carmarthen dep	6 15	1130	...	...	6 30
Neath ....dep	8 35	1 40	4 50	8 40	8 30
Aberdylais	8 40	1 45	4 55	8 45	8 35
Resolven	8 50	1 55	5 5	8 55	8 45
Glyn-Neath	8 58	2 5	5 13	9 3	8 53
Hirwain	9 23	2 28	5 38	9 28	9 18
Merthyr Road	9 27	2 33	5 42	9 32	9 22
Merthyr* ... arr	1035	3 40	6 50	1040	1030
Aberdare ...... „	9 35	2 40	5 50	9 40	9 30

* The distance between Merthyr Road Station and Merthyr is run by Omnibus. Fare, 1s.

Coaches from Merthyr for Abergavenny, Nantyglo, Brynmawr, Tredegar, Rhymney, Dowlais, Brecon, Builth and the Llanwrtyd and Llandrindod Wells; and from Carmarthen for Tenby and Aberystwyth.

January 1853

MERTHYR, ABERDARE, HIRWAIN, and NEATH.—Vale of Neath.

Miles	Fares 1st class	2nd class	3rd class	Down.	Wk Days 1 2 3 class	1 2 3 class	1 2 3 class	Sun. 1 2 3 class	1 2 3 class
	s. d.	s. d.	s. d.		mrn	aft	aft	mrn	aft
—	...	...	...	**Merthyr** ......dep	9 0	1 50	6 0	9 0	6 30
— 1	2 0	1 0	0 5½	Llwydcoed	9 15	2 5	6 15	9 15	6 45
2¼	[illegible]	[illegible]	[illegible]	**Aberdare** ... dep	9 5	1 55	6 5	9 5	6 35
3¼	1 6	1 0	0 7½	**Hirwain** Junc ...	9 26	2 16	6 26	9 26	6 56
14	2 10	1 10	1 2	Glyn-Neath	9 47	2 37	6 47	9 47	7 17
16¾	3 4	2 2	1 4½	Resolven	9 56	2 46	6 56	9 56	7 26
21¼	4 2	2 8	1 9	Aberdylais	10 5	2 55	7 5	10 5	7 35
23	4 6	3 0	1 11	**Neath**...p. 16 ....arr	1010	3 0	7 10	1010	7 40
60¼	11 3	[illegible]	5 0	Carmarthen arr	1230	4 50	9 35	1220	10 0

Up.	Wk Days 1 2 3 class	1 2 3 class	1 2 3 class	Sun. 1 2 3 class	1 2 3 class
	mrn	mrn	aft	mrn	aft
Carmarthen dep	6 15	1020	5 45	7 15	6 30
Neath ....dep.	8 35	1 40	7 40	9 20	[illegible]
Aberdylais	8 40	1 45	7 45	9 25	[illegible]
Resolven	8 50	1 55	7 55	9 33	[illegible]
Glyn-Neath	8 59	2 3	8 3	9 43	[illegible]
Hirwain June ...	9 20	2 25	8 25	10 3	[illegible]
Aberdare ...arr	9 30	2 35	8 35	1025	[illegible]
Merthyr Road.........	9 35	2 40	8 40	1029	[illegible]
Merthyr ......arr	9 50	2 55	8 55	1035	9 45

Extra.—Aberdare to Hirwain, at 8 10 aft. SUNDAYS at 5 30 aft. Hirwain to Aberdare, at 8½ aft. SUNDAYS at 7 aft.
Coaches from Merthyr for Dowlais, Rhymney, Tredegar, Brynmawr, Abergavenny, Brecon, Builth, &c.; and from Carmarthen for Tenby, Aberystwyth, &c.

December 1853

PONTYPOOL ROAD, QUAKER'S YARD, MERTHYR, ABERDARE, NEATH, & SWANSEA.—G.W.

Week Days (columns 1–19), Sundays (columns S1–S2).

Miles from Pontypool Rd.	Down.	1 mrn	2 mrn	3 mrn (Rail Motor Car. One class only.)	4 mrn	5 mrn (Rail Motor Car. One class only.)	6 mrn (Runs on the 21st, 23rd, 28th, and 30th instant.)	7 mrn	8 mrn (Rail Motor Car. One class only.)	9 mrn	10 aft (Rail Motor Car. One class only.)	11 aft (Rail Motor Car. One class only.)	12 mrn	13 mrn	14 aft (Rail Motor Car. One class only.)	15 aft	16 aft (Rail Motor Car. One class only.)	17 mrn	18 aft	19 aft	S1 mrn	S2 aft
	68 London (Paddington) dp	....	....	....	....	....		....	....	....	....	....	5 40	....	....	....	....	1020	1 45	1 50	....	....
	68 Birmingham (S.H.) „	....	....	....	....	....		....	....	8d5	....	....	1015	1135	....	....	....	1147	4 0	5 50	....	12 5
	68 Worcester (ShrbH.) „	....	....	....	....	....		....	....	7c25	....	b	1120	1240	b	....	....	2 22	5 b 5	7 b 0	....	1b20
	68 Hereford (Barr'sC.) „	3i53	....	....	....	....		7 15	....	9n10	....	....	1242	1 55	....	....	....	4 15	6 38	8 5	3 53	2 23
—	**Pontypool Road** ......dep.	7 20	....		7 50			8 55		1050			2 14	3 25		....		6 20	7 50	9 30	8 55	5 0
2½	**Pontypool * 87, 425**	7 26	....		7 56			9 1		1058			2 20	3 33		....		6 28	7 56	9 38	9 1	5 6
6	Crumlin (High Level) † 87.	7 40	....		8 10			9 16		1114			2 35	3 48		....		6 43	8 10	9 53	9 16	5 21
8¾	Pontllanfraith ....[424	7g45	....		8 16			9 25		1120			2 41	3 54		....		6 49	8 16	9 59	9 22	5 27
10¾	Hengoed & Maesycwmmer..	—	....		8 22			9 35		1129			2 47	4 0		....		6 55	8 23	10 5	9 31	5 36
13½	Llancaiach 500	Stop	....		8 29			9 43		1136			2 54	4 7		....		7 2	8 30	1013	9 38	5 43
15	Treharris	....	....		8 34			9 48		1141			2 59	4 12		....		7 7	8 35	1018	9 43	5 48
15¾	**Quaker's Yard** (H.L.) 93 ..	....	....		8 37			9 51		1144			3 2	4 15		....		7 10	8 38	1021	9 46	5 51
18	Aberfan, for Merthyr Vale	....	....		8 49			10 6		1157			....	4 26		....		7 21	9 1	1032	9 56	6 1
21	Abercanaid	....	....		....			1013		12 4			....	....		....		7 29	9 8	1039	10 4	6 9
22½	**Merthyr 425** ....arr.	....	....		9 0			1019		1210			....	4 38		....		7 36	9 14	1045	1010	6 15
17½	Penrhiwceiber 90	mrn	....		8 47			10 0		1152			3 10	4 23		....		7 19	....	....	9 53	5 59
19¼	Mountain Ash	7 25	....		8 53		9 40	10 5		1157			3 15	4 27		....		7 23	8 47	1040	9 58	6 4
22¼	**Aberdare**	7 33	....		9 5		9 50	1015		12 6			3 25	4 35		5 45		7 33	8 56	1051	10 7	6 14
26	Hirwain 83	7 47	....	....	9 21	....	1010	1029	....	1220	....	....	3 39	....	....	5 56	....	7 48	9 7	11 0	1019	6 27
32¼	Glyn Neath	8 0	....	....	9 35	9 57	....	1044	1145	1235	2 5	....	3 52	....	5 25	6 11	7 17	8 4	9 22	Saturdays only.	1034	6 42
35¼	Resolven	8 6	....	....	9 41	10 4	....	1050	1152	1242	2 12	....	3 59	....	5 32	6 18	7 24	8 11	9 29		1040	6 48
39¾	Aberdylais	8 18	....	....	9 51	1017	....	1059	12 5	1251	2 25	....	4 8	....	5 45	6 27	7 37	8 21	....		1049	6 57
41½	**Neath** (Town Sta.) 78, 608	8 30	8 40	....	9 59	....	1043	11 7	....	1 2	....	....	4 14	....	....	6 31	....	8 29	9 44		1055	7 4
—	**Neath** (Low Level)...dep.	Arr. Neath at 8 24 mrn.	....	8 30	....	1022	To Carmarthen.	....	1210	1 15	2 30	3 50	....	....	5 50	....	7 42	....	....		....	....
42½	Neath Abbey		....	8 33	....	1026		....	1214	1 19	2 34	3 53	....	....	5 54	....	7 46	....	....		....	....
45¼	Briton Ferry Road		....	8 41	....	1034		....	1222	1 26	2 42	4 1	....	....	6 2	....	7 54	....	....		....	....
48¼	**Swansea** (East Dock) arr.		....	8 49	....	1042		....	1230	1 33	2 50	4 9	....	....	6 10	....	8 2	....	....		....	....
43¾	Skewen		8 49					1116	....	1 11	....	....	4 23			6 49	....	8 38	....	....	11 4	7 13
45¼	Llansamlet		8 55	....	....	....		1122	....	1 17	....	....	4 30	....	....	6 55	....	8 44	....	....	1110	7 19
48	Landore (*see below*)	8 45	9 3	....	....	....		1133	....	1 28	....	....	4 39	....	....	7 3	....	8 53	10 3	....	1116	7 28
49¼	**Swansea** (High St.) 423 arr.	9 2	9 10	....	1015	....		1140	....	1 35	....	....	4 46	....	....	7 10	....	9 0	1010	....	1128	7 35

b Foregate Street. *c* Leaves Foregate Street at 9 5 mrn. on Mondays. *d* Mondays only. *g* Tuesdays only. *h* Thursdays only. *i* Except Mondays. *n* Leaves at 9 49 mrn. on Mondays. *s* Saturdays only. * Clarence Street Station. † About ¾ mile to Low Level Station. "**Halts**" at Melyncourt and Clyne, between Resolven and Aberdylais, and at Cardonnel, between Neath Abbey and Briton Ferry Road.

July 1906

PONTYPOOL ROAD, MERTHYR, ABERDARE, NEATH, and SWANSEA.—Great Western.

Week Days (columns 1–22), Suns. (columns S1–S2).

Mls. frm Pon. Rd.	Down.	1 mrn	2 mrn	3 mrn	4 mrn	5 mrn	6 mrn	7 mrn	8 mrn	9 mrn	10 aft	11 aft	12 mrn	13 mrn	14 aft	15 aft	16 aft	17 aft	18 aft	19 aft	20 aft	21 aft	22	S1 mrn	S2 aft
	Paddington Station, 102 London ....dep.	....	....	....	....	....	1k0	....	....	5 30	....	....	9 0	1130	....	....	....	1 10	....	3 35	4 30	....	....	1 0	....
—	**Pontypool Road** .....dep.	....	7 20	....	....	....	7 50	8 55	....	11 0	....	....	2 14	3 25	....	....	....	6 25	....	7 50	9 40	....	....	8 55	5 0
1	Pontypool * 73, 474	....	7 26	....	....	....	7 56	9 1	....	11 8	....	....	2 20	3 33	....	....	....	6 32	....	7 56	9 48	....	....	9 1	5 6
6	Crumlin (High Level) † 75	....	7 40	....	....	....	8 10	9 16	....	1123	....	....	2 35	3 48	....	....	....	6 47	....	8 10	10 3	....	....	9 16	5 21
8¾	Pontllanfraith 472....[98	....	7g45	....	....	....	8 16	9 25	....	1129	....	....	2 41	3 54	....	....	....	6 55	Saturdays only.	8 16	10 9	....	....	9 22	5 27
10¾	Hengoed & Maesycwmmer	....	....	....	....	....	8 22	9 35	....	1139	....	....	2 47	4 0	....	....	....	7 2		8 23	1015	....	....	9 31	5 36
13½	Nelson & Llancaiach 98, 99 arr.	....	....	....	....	....	8 27	9 41	....	1145	....	....	2 53	4 6	....	....	....	7 8		8 29	1021	....	....	9 37	5 42
	Nelson & Llancaiach dep.	....	....	....	....	....	8 29	9 43	....	1146	....	....	2 54	4 7	....	....	....	7 10		8 31	1022	....	....	9 38	5 43
15	Treharris ....[119	....	....	....	....	....	8 34	9 48	....	1151	....	....	2 59	4 12	....	....	....	7 15		8 36	1027	....	....	9 43	5 48
15¾	Quaker's Yard (H.L.) 98, ar	....	....	....	....	....	8 37	9 51	....	1154	....	....	3 2	4 15	....	....	....	7 18		8 39	1030	....	....	9 46	5 51
22¾	98 Merthyr ....arr.	....	....	....	....	....	9 2	1022	m	1225	....	....	3 50	4 40	....	....	m	7 50		9 19	11 0	....	....	1010	6 15
—	Quaker's Yard (H.L.)..dep	....	....	....	....	....	8 41	9 54	11 5	1157	....	....	3 4	4 17	....	....	6 20	7 22		8 41	1032	1053	....	9 48	5 53
17½	Penrhiwceiber 117	....	....	....	....	....	8 47	10 0	1111	12 2	....	....	3 10	4 23	....	....	6 26	7 28		8 47	....	....	....	9 53	5 59
18¾	Mountain Ash	....	....	....	....	m	8 53	10 5	1115	12 7	m	m	3 15	4 27	....	....	6 30	7 33	m	8 52	1039	11 1	....	9 58	6 4
22½	**Aberdare** ¶	7 30	....	....	....	8 50	9 5	1015	1127	1219	1 22	2 45	3 25	4 35	....	5 50	6 42	7 44	8 40	9 4	1048	1110	....	10 7	6 14
26	Hirwain ¶ 71 ...... arr.	7 38	....	....	....	9 1	9 15	1024	1138	1227	1 33	2 56	3 34	....	....	5 58	6 53	7 52	8 59	9 12		1125 s		1016	6 23
	Hirwain dep.	7 44	....	....	....	9 2	9 21	1029	1139	1233	1 34	2 59	3 39	....	m	6 1	6 54	7 58	9 2	9 16	Saturdays only.	....	....	1019	6 27
32¼	Glyn Neath	7 57	....	....	....	9 20	9 35	1044	1157	1247	1 52	3 17	3 52	....	5 20	6 16	7 12	8 11	Runs to Pontwalby Halt.	9 31		....	....	1034	6 42
35¼	Resolven ¶	8 3	....	....	....	9 27	9 41	1050	12 4	1254	1 59	3 24	3 59	....	5 27	6 23	7 19	8 18		9 38		....	....	1040	6 48
39¾	Aberdylais	8 15	....	....	....	9 40	9 51	1059	1217	1 3	2 12	3 37	4 8	....	5 40	6 32	7 32	8 28		....		....	....	1049	6 57
41½	**Neath** (Town) 64, 619 arr.	8 24	....	....	m	....	9 58	11 9	....	1 15	....	....	4 13	....		6 36	....	8 37		9 54		....	....	1059	7 3
—	Neath (Low Level)..dep.	....	....	....	8 30	9 44	....	....	1222	1 24	2 18	3 42	....	....	5 45	....	7 37	....		....		....	....	....	....
42¾	Neath Abbey ¶	....	....	....	8 34	9 48	....	....	1226	1 28	2 22	3 46	....	....	5 50	....	7s41	....		....		....	....	....	....
45¼	Briton Ferry Road	....	....	....	8 42	9 55	....	....	1234	1 35	2 30	3 53	....	....	5 58	....	7s49	....		....		....	....	....	....
48¼	Swansea (East Dock) arr	....	....	....	8 49	10 2	....	....	1242	1 42	2 37	4 0	....	....	6 5	....	7s56	....		....		....	....	....	....
—	**Neath** (Town).......dep.	8 30	....	8 42	....	....	9 59	1110	....	1 16	....	....	4 14	....		6 48	....	8 38		9 55	....	....	....	11 0	7 4
43¾	Skewen	....	....	8 50	....	....	....	1117	....	1 23	....	....	4 23	....	....	6 55	....	8 45		Th.	....	....	....	11 5	....
45¾	Llansamlet	....	....	8 58	....	....	....	1124	....	1 30	....	....	4 30	....	....	7 2	....	8 52		Th.	....	....	....	1112	....
48	Landore 60, 79	8 57	....	9 10	....	....	....	1140	....	1 40	....	....	4 41	....	....	7 15	....	9 2	....	1015	....	....	....	1130	7 22
49¼	Swansea (High St.) 472 arr	9 2	....	9 15	....	....	1015	1145	....	1 45	....	....	4 46	....	....	7 20	....	9 7	....	1020	....	....	....	1135	7 27

g Tuesdays only. *k* Except Monday mornings. **m** Motor Car, one class only. *s* Saturdays only.

NOTES.

* Clarence Street Station.
† About ¾ mile to Low Level Station.
¶ "Halts" at Trecynon, between Aberdare and Hirwain; Rhigos and Pontwalby, between Hirwain and Glyn Neath; Melyncourt and Clyne, between Resolven and Aberdylais; and Cardonnel, between Neath Abbey and Briton Ferry Road.

October 1912

PONTYPOOL ROAD, CARDIFF, MERTHYR, NEATH, and SWANSEA.

Miles from Pontypool Rd	Down	Week Days only.																													
		mrn	mrn	mrn	mrn	mrn	mrn	mrn	mrn	mrn	mrn	mrn	mrn	aft	aft	mrn		mrn	aft	aft	aft	aft	aft	aft	aft	aft	aft	aft	aft	aft	aft
															S	③				E		E					E		S	S	E
	125London (Pad.)....... dep	..	..	..	..	1255	..	..	..	..	..	..	5 30	..	..	..	..	9 15	..	③	..	..	..	..	..	1 55	..	3U55	..	..	..
	125Bristol (T.M.) 64... "	..	..	..	..	5 50	..	..	..	..	..	..	9 5	..	..	9 5	..	12 37	..	..	..	..	..	..	..	4 40	..	5 0	..	..	..
	125Newport .... "	..	③	..	..	7 16	..	③	..	..	7 55	..	10 10	..	..	1040	..	1 33	..	..	..	..	..	..	..	5 35	..	6 49	..	..	..
	Pontypool Road ...... dep	Workmen's Train.	6 40	..	..	7 45	..	8 16	..	..	8 40	..	11 0	..	..	1 15	..	2 28	..	4 0	..	..	..	..	..	6 20	..	7 50	..	..	..
1¼	Pontypool A 80...........		6 44	..	..	7 50	..	8 20	..	..	8 45	..	11 5	..	..	1 19	..	2 33	..	4 5	..	..	..	..	..	6 25	..	7 55	..	..	..
5½	Hafodyrynys Platform.....		6 56	..	..	8 0	..	8 30	..	..	8 57	..	11 15	..	..	1 29	..	2 42	..	4 15	..	..	..	..	..	6 34	..	8 5	..	..	..
6¼	Crumlin (H. Level) B ¶ 81		7 0	..	..	8 5	..	8 34	..	..	9 1	..	11 20	..	..	1 33	..	2 47	..	4 21	..	..	..	..	..	6 39	..	8 9	..	..	..
7¾	Pentwynmawr Platform...		7 4	..	..	8 9	..	8 40	..	..	9 5	..	11 24	..	..	1 37	..	2 50	..	4 27	..	..	..	..	..	6 42	..	8 14	..	..	..
9½	Penmaen Halt........ arr		..	..	..	..	..	..	..	..	..	..	..	..	..	..	..	..	..	..	..	..	..	..	..	..	..	..	..	..	..
9	Pontllanfraith C 503, 504..	..	7 9	..	..	8 12	..	8 43	..	..	9 7	..	11 27	..	..	1 40	..	2 53	..	4 30	..	..	..	..	..	6 45	..	8 17	..	..	..
11	Hengoed (High Level) D...	6 17	7 14	..	..	8 17	..	8 47	..	..	9 12	..	11 36	..	..	1 45	..	3 0	..	4 36	..	..	..	..	..	6 49	..	8 23	..	..	..
14	Nelson & Llancaiach 89 arr	6 23	7 29	..	..	8 23	..	..	..	..	9 18	③	11 42	..	..	1 50	..	3 5	③	4 42	..	..	..	..	..	6 55	..	8 29	③	..	..
—	Mls Cardiff (Queen St)¶dp	5H12	..	6 38	..	..	..	Except Saturdays and School Holidays	8 18	..	..	10 8	10H55	..	..	..	..	1H55	3 15	3H40	..	4 35	..	5 0	..	5H30	..	7H30	8 33	..	..
—	3½ Llanishen ¶...........	5H21	..	6 48		..	..		8 28	..	..	1018	11 H5	..	..	..	..	2 H5	3 25	3H50	..	4 45	..	5 10	③	5H42	..	7H40	8 43	..	..
—	7 Caerphilly.............	5H36	..	7 2	..	..	..		8 38	..	..	1029	11H16	..	..	..	..	2H18	3 37	4 H5	..	4 56	..	5 20	5 26	5H55	..	7H51	8 55	..	..
—	9½ Llanbradach...........	5H43	..	7 10	③	..	..		8 45	..	..	1036	11H22	..	..	..	..	2H27	3 43	4H13	..	5 4	③	..	5 32	6 H4	..	8 H0	9 1	..	..
—	12½ Ystrad Mynach.....[89	5H52	..	7 18	7 20	..	..		8 51	8 55	..	1043	11H28	..	1235	..	..	2H34	3 51	4H20	..	5 10	5 16	..	5 39	6H11	..	8 H6	9 9	..	..
—	14½ Nelson & Llancaiach ar	..	..	..	7 26	..	..		..	9 0	..	1046	..	..	1239	..	..	..	3 56	..	..	..	5 20	..	5 43	..	..	..	9 14	..	..
—	Nelson & Llancaiach ¶ dep	..	..	..	7 28	8 24	..		..	..	9 19	1048	11 43	..	1240	1 51	..	3 6	3 59	4 47	Except Saturdays and School Holidays.	—	5 21	..	5 44	6 56	..	8 30	9 15	..	..
15½	Treharris ....[84	..	..	..	7 34	8 30	..		..	..	9 25	1053	11 49	..	1245	1 56	..	3 11	4 5	4 53		..	5 26	..	5 49	7 1	..	8 36	9 20	..	..
16	Quaker's Yard (H.L.) F arr	..	..	..	7 36	8 32	③		..	..	9 27	1055	11 51	③	1247	1 58	..	3 13	4 7	4 55		..	5 28	..	5 51	7 2	③	8 39	9 22	..	..
—	Mls Quaker's Yd (H.L) ¶dp	..	..	..	..	..	8 40		..	..	..	11 0	..	1210	..	..	..	..	4 8	..		..	..	..	5 52	..	7 15	..	9 23	..	..
—	2¼ Aberfan ¶.............	..	..	..	..	..	8 47		..	..	..	11 7	..	1218	..	..	..	..	4 15	..		..	..	..	5 59	..	7 22	..	9 30	..	..
—	5¼ Abercanaid	..	..	..	..	..	8 56		..	..	..	1116	..	1226	..	..	..	..	4 23	..		..	..	..	6 8	..	7 31	..	9 39	..	..
—	7 Merthyr 486 ...... arr	..	..	..	..	..	9 1		..	..	..	1121	..	1232	..	..	..	..	4 29	..		..	..	..	6 13	..	7 36	..	9 44	..	..
—	Quaker's Yard (H.L.).. dep	..	..	..	7 37	8 35	..	..	..	..	9 30	..	11 54	..	1248	2 2	..	3 16	..	4 58		..	5 29	..	..	7 3	..	8 41	..	..	..
17¾	Penrhiwceiber (H.L.) 89....	..	..	..	7 41	8 40	..	..	..	..	9 34	..	11 59	..	1252	2 7	..	3 21	..	5 3		..	5 34	..	..	7 8	..	8 46	..	..	..
19	Mountain Ash (Cardiff Rd.)	..	..	..	7 45	8 44	..	..	..	..	9 38	..	12 3	..	1256	2 10	..	3 24	..	5 7		..	5 37	..	..	7 12	..	8 50	..	..	..
21½	Cwmbach Halt............	..	..	..	7 49	..	..	..	..	..	9 42	..	12 7	..	1 0	2 14	..	3 31	..	5 11		..	..	..	..	7 17	..	..	..	..	..
22¾	Aberdare (H.L.) ¶... arr	..	..	..	7 53	8 52	..	..	..	..	9 46	..	12 12	..	1 5	2 18	..	3 34	..	5 15		..	5 48	..	..	7 21	..	8 58	..	..	..
	Aberdare (H.L.) ¶... dep	..	..	..	8 5	..	..	..	..	..	9 47	..	12 15	..	..	2 20	..	3 38	..	..		..	..	..	..	7 33	..	..	..	..	..
26½	Hirwaun 96........... arr	..	..	..	8 15	..	..	..	..	..	9 58	..	12 23	..	..	2 32	..	3 48	..	..	③	..	..	..	..	7 45	..	..	..	..	..
—	96 Merthyr .... dep	..	..	..	7 45	..	..	..	..	..	9T30	..	11T53	..	..	2 0	..	3T19	..	..	4 54	..	..	..	..	7T15	..	..	..	..	..
—	Hirwaun ¶ .... dep	..	..	..	8 16	..	..	..	..	..	10 0	..	12 25	..	..	2 33	..	3 52	..	..	5 15	..	..	..	..	7 47	..	..	..	..	..
32¾	Glyn Neath................	..	..	..	8 34	..	..	..	..	..	1014	..	12 39	..	..	2 51	..	4 6	..	..	5 33	..	..	..	..	8 1	..	..	..	1025	1115
35¾	Resolven ¶................	..	..	..	8 40	..	..	..	..	..	1020	..	12 45	..	..	2 57	..	4 12	..	..	..	..	..	..	..	8 7	..	..	..	1030	1122
40	Aberdylais................	..	..	..	8 51	..	..	..	..	..	1032	..	12 53	..	..	3 9	..	4 21	..	..	..	..	..	..	..	8 15	..	..	..	1039	1137
41¾	Neath (Gen) 64, 69, 89 ar	..	..	..	8L55	..	..	..	..	..	1036	..	12 57	..	..	3 13	..	4 25	..	..	..	..	..	..	..	8 20	..	..	..	1043	1141
49½	64 Swansea (High St.) arr	..	..	..	9 42	..	..	..	..	..	1112	..	1 39	..	..	4 2	..	4 51	..	..	..	..	..	..	..	9 12	..	..	..	11 3	4a31

A Clarence Street, about ¼ mile to Crane Street Station. a Mrn. B About ¼ mile to Low Level Sta. C About ¼ mile to L. M.&S. Sta.
D Adjoining Hengoed (L. L.) Sta. and about ¼ mile to Maesycwmmer Station. E or E Except Saturdays. F Adjoins Low Level Station. H Via Hengoed
L Neath (Riverside Sta.). S or S Sats only T Third class only. U Fris. only ③ Third class only.

May 1944

September 1962

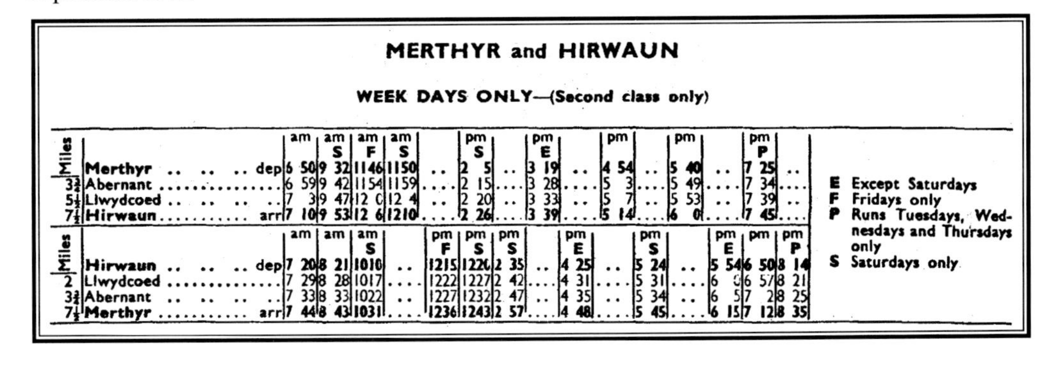

MERTHYR and HIRWAUN

WEEK DAYS ONLY—(Second class only)

Miles		am	am	am	am		pm		pm		pm		pm		pm	
			S	F	S		S		E						P	
	Merthyr .. .. .. dep	**6 50**	**9 32**	**1146**	**1150**	..	**2 5**	..	**3 19**	..	**4 54**	..	**5 40**	..	**7 25**	..
3¾	Abernant	6 59	9 42	1154	1159	....	2 15	....	3 28	....	5 3	....	5 49	....	7 34	....
5½	Llwydcoed	7 3	9 47	12 0	12 4	..	2 20	..	3 33	..	5 7	..	5 53	..	7 39	..
7½	**Hirwaun** .... arr	**7 10**	**9 53**	**12 6**	**1210**	....	**2 26**	....	**3 39**	....	**5 14**	....	**6 0**	....	**7 45**	....

Miles		am	am	am		pm	pm	pm		pm		pm		pm	pm	pm
				S		F	S	S		E		S		E		P
	Hirwaun .. .. .. dep	**7 20**	**8 21**	**1010**	..	**1215**	**1220**	**2 35**	..	**4 25**	..	**5 24**	..	**5 54**	**6 50**	**8 14**
2	Llwydcoed	7 29	8 28	1017	....	1222	1227	2 42	....	4 31	....	5 31	....	6 0	6 57	8 21
3¾	Abernant	7 33	8 33	1022	..	1227	1232	2 47	..	4 35	..	5 34	..	6 5	7 2	8 25
7½	**Merthyr** .... arr	**7 44**	**8 43**	**1031**	....	**1236**	**1243**	**2 57**	....	**4 48**	....	**5 45**	....	**6 15**	**7 12**	**8 35**

E Except Saturdays
F Fridays only
P Runs Tuesdays, Wednesdays and Thursdays only
S Saturdays only

MOUNTAIN ASH (CARDIFF ROAD)

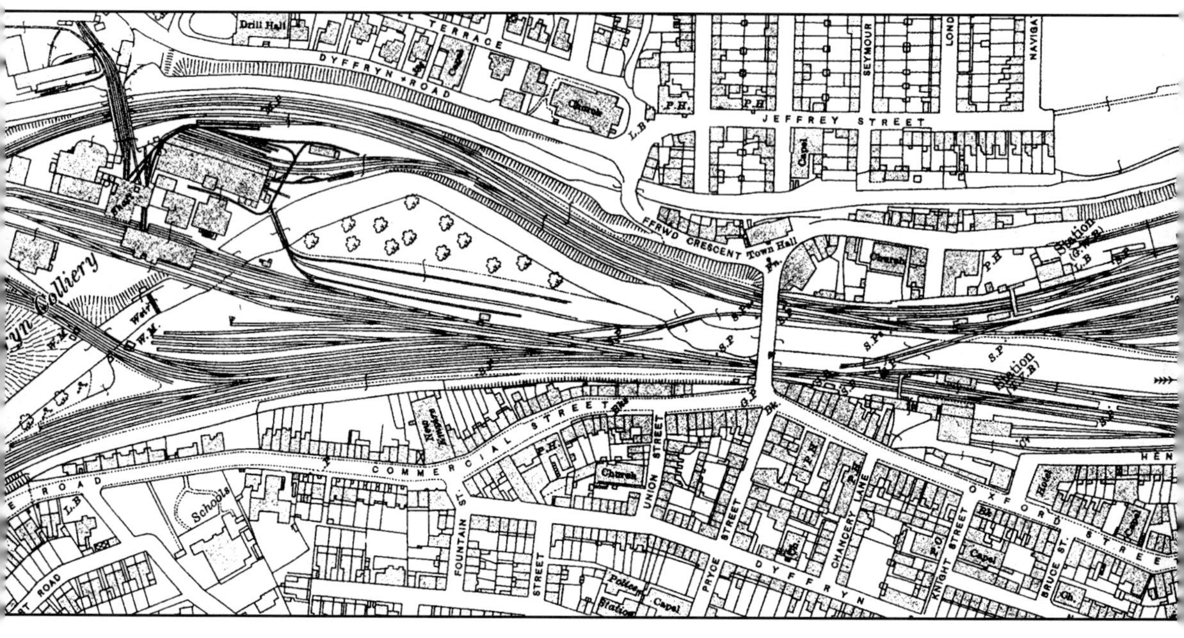

III. The 1921 map has the GWR route from Pontypool Road on the right, with colliery lines diverging from it. At the bottom of the right page is the Taff Vale Railway; the two stations are on the right of the left page. A new station was opened on the site of the TVR one in 1988.

1. This postcard view is towards Neath from a position near the join of the pages and shows the GWR station before it received the suffix "Cardiff Road" on 1st July 1924. The TVR station became "Oxford Street"; both closed to passengers in 1964. (R.H.Marrows coll.)

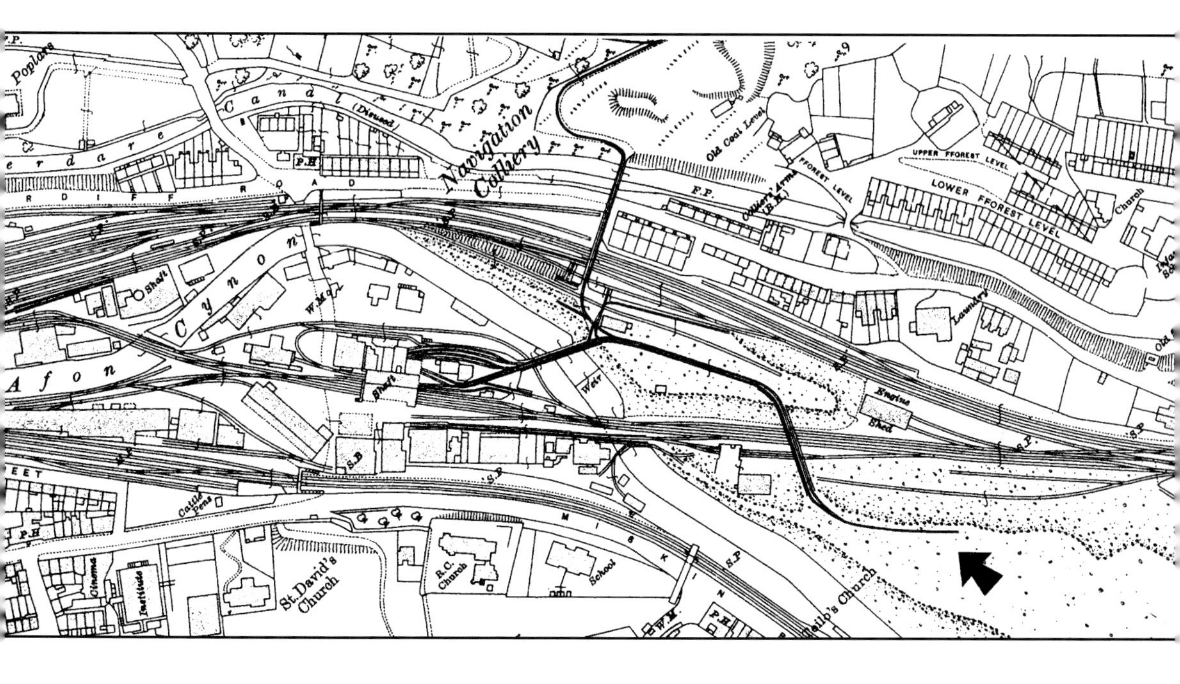

2. A view in the other direction in June 1922 has the GWR tracks to the left of the 30-lever signal box and colliery lines to the right of it. The building in the background (centre) later became the National Coal Board locomotive shed. (D.K.Jones coll.)

3. Obscured by the footbridge in the previous photograph is Cresselly level crossing and the public footbridge. They pass over three lines, but the gates span only two. The third was a colliery track and it passed under a bridge span of different design. The lamp has one red glass as a warning that there are gates nearby. These carried no lights or warning discs. (G.Davis/B.King coll.)

4. The river is in the foreground as 0-6-2T no. 5633 heads a class K freight, bound for Aberdare, on 12th January 1960. The ringed signal is for goods engines joining the BR down line. (S.Rickard/J&J coll.)

5. The Afon Cynon was in flood on 9th March 1963 after a period of exceptionally prolonged snowfall, but it did not deter the driver of 0-6-2T no. 6622, when arriving from Neath. (C.Gifford)

6. Like picture no. 4, this shot was taken from the road bridge over the railway and the river. Here is the scene on 28th October 1974 after the NCB had taken over the former GWR track and built a weighbridge office on the site of the platform lines. Andrew Barclay 0-6-0T no. 2074 *Llantanam Abbey* is in the foreground, while NCB no. 1 (a Hudswell Clark 0-6-0ST) is in the background. (T.Heavyside)

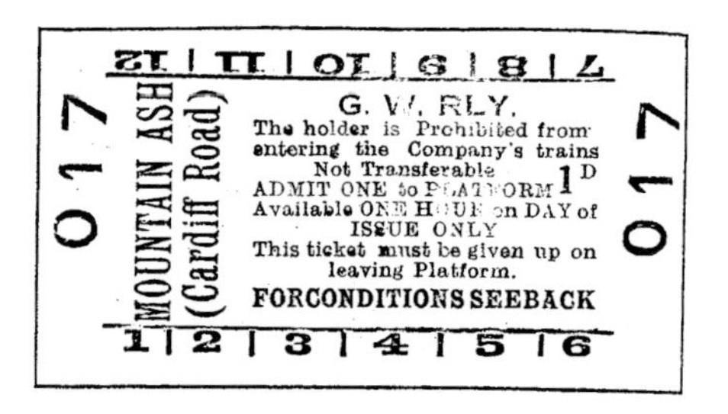

NORTH OF MOUNTAIN ASH

7. A view up the left border of the map features Deep Duffryn Colliery. The GWR passed behind it and it had a second connection to the sidings, beyond the left of this picture, from about 1910 to 1948. (R.H.Marrows coll.)

8. A train from Neath approaches the station behind 2-6-2T no. 5103 on 12th January 1960. In the foreground is the eastern connection to Deep Duffryn Colliery, which was in use from 1850 to 1979. The next picture is from the same bridge. (S.Rickard/J&J coll.)

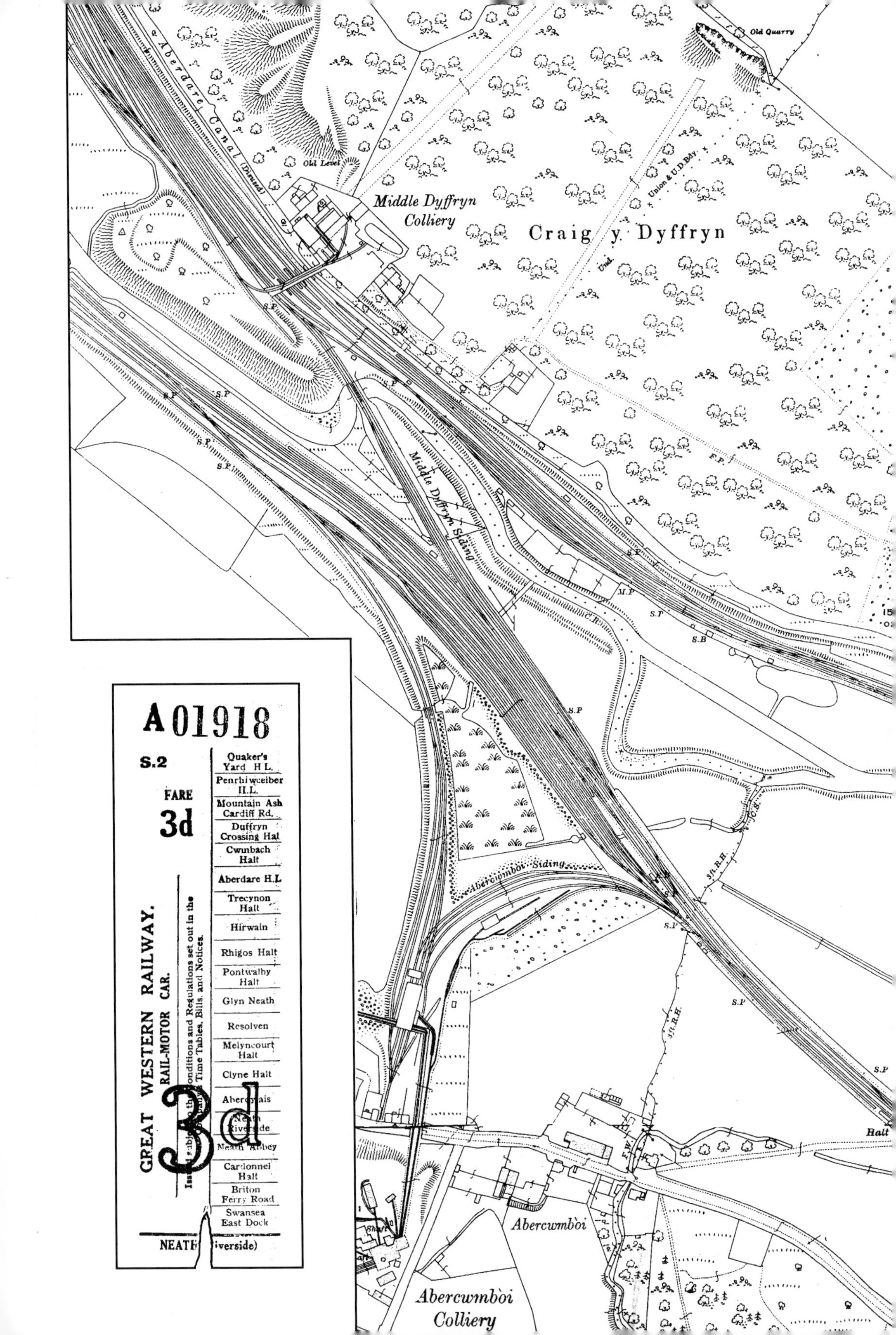
Old Quarry
Aberdare Canal (Disused)
Old Level
Middle Dyffryn Colliery
Craig y Dyffryn
Union & U.D. Bdy.
Und.
F.P.
S.P
M.P
S.B
C.R
Middle Dyffryn Siding
Abercwmboi Siding
Halt
F.W.
Shaft
Abercwmboi
Abercwmboi Colliery
A 01918
S.2
FARE
3d
GREAT WESTERN RAILWAY.
RAIL-MOTOR CAR.
Quaker's Yard H.L.
Penrhiwceiber H.L.
Mountain Ash Cardiff Rd.
Duffryn Crossing Hal
Cwmbach Halt
Aberdare H.L
Trecynon Halt
Hirwain
Rhigos Halt
Pontwalby Halt
Glyn Neath
Resolven
Melyncourt Halt
Clyne Halt
Cardonnel Halt
Briton Ferry Road
Swansea East Dock

9. The NCB used the former BR lines to Middle Duffryn from 1971 to 1987. This load of coal was bound for the Phurnacite plant at Aberamen on 5th October 1971, but had stalled and is running back for another attempt. No. 7754 is providing banking assistance to a diesel. (T.Heavyside)

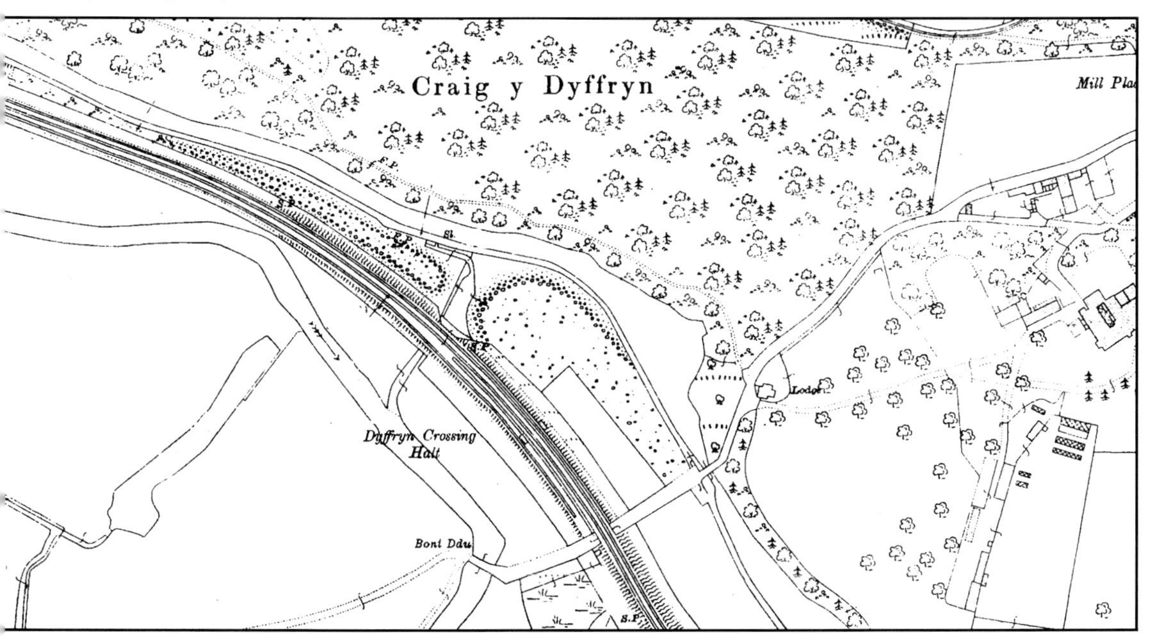

IV. Abercwmboi Halt is lower right on the left page of this 1919 map and is on the TVR. On the right page is GWR's Duffryn Crossing Halt, which was open only from 12th July 1914 to 2nd April 1917. Middle Duffryn Colliery did not raise coal after 1885, but became a central washery and despatched good steam coal into the 1970s. Abercwmboi Colliery had no direct connection with our route. The Middle Duffryn - Aberdare section closed on 29th November 1971.

10. Middle Duffryn sidings were being shunted by no. 08484 on 27th June 1980. Smoke and dust still prevailed from the adjacent Phurnacite plant. (P.Jones)

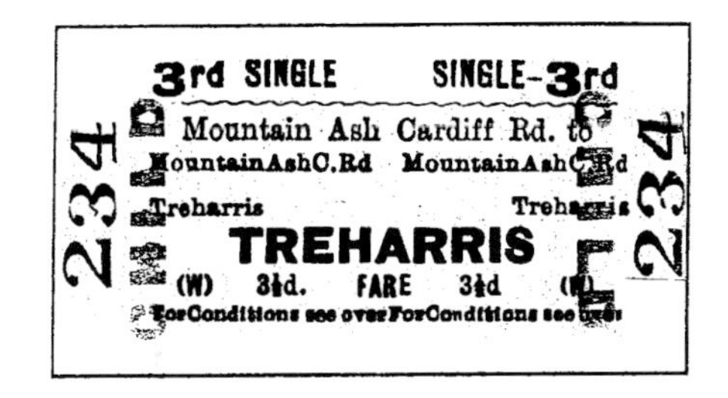

CWMBACH HALT

11. This halt opened on 12th July 1914 for the benefit of workers at several collieries. This view towards Mountain Ash is from July 1963. (P.J.Garland/R.S.Carpenter coll.)

12. A connection from the TVR crossed the GWR route on the level here until 4th July 1943. It served Werfa Colliery, Upper Duffryn Colliery and Cwmbach Pit and was replaced by a link with Lletty Shenkin Colliery, the sidings of which were parallel to the GWR. The 1910 signal box was named after the colliery and closed officially on 15th June 1964. It is seen in June 1963, boarded up before official closure. (R.H.Marrows)

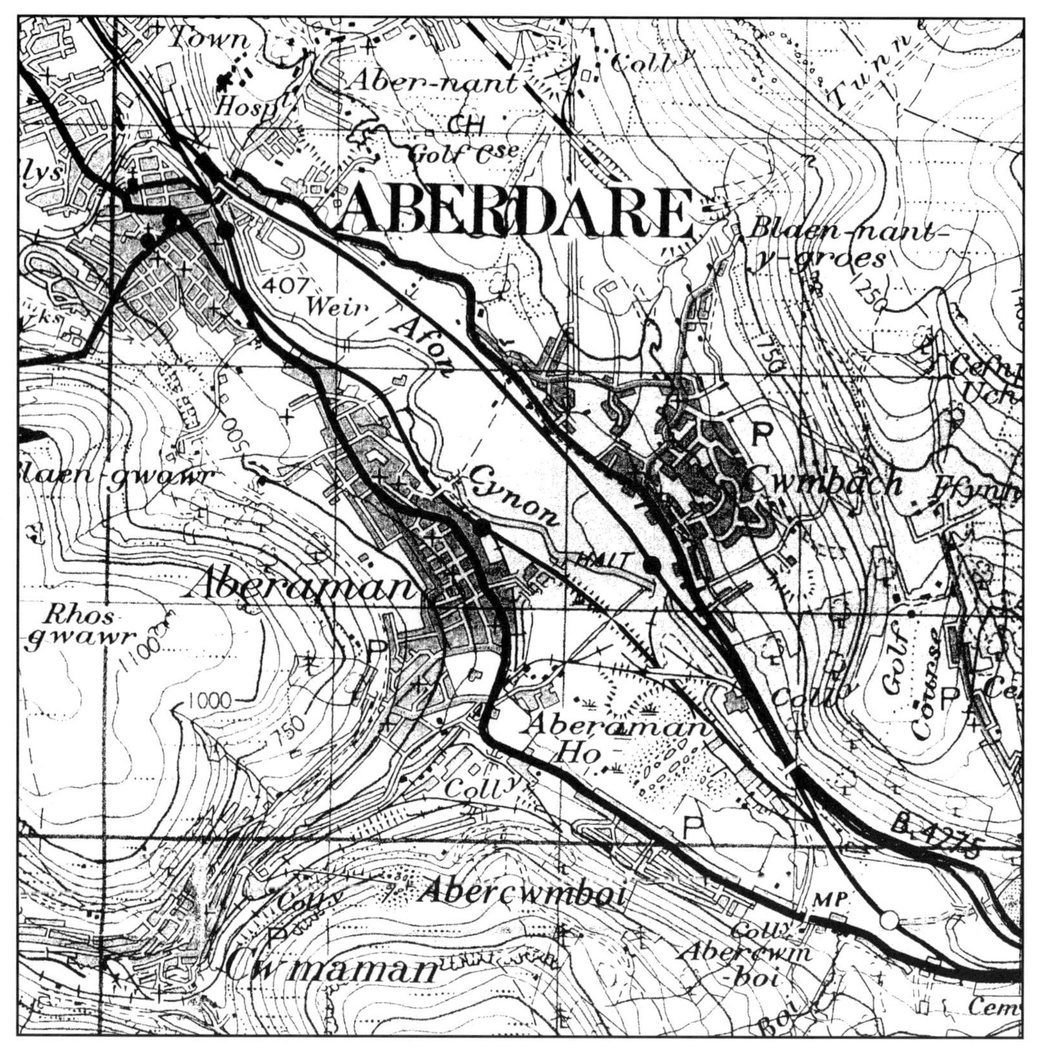

V. The TVR trackbed from here northward was required for a new road and so the connection just mentioned was relaid, the new track coming into use on 29th July 1973. When passenger service to Aberdare was reinstated in 1988, a platform was provided on the site of Cwmbach Halt, but it was named simply Cwmbach. The map is at 2ins to 1 mile and is from 1954.

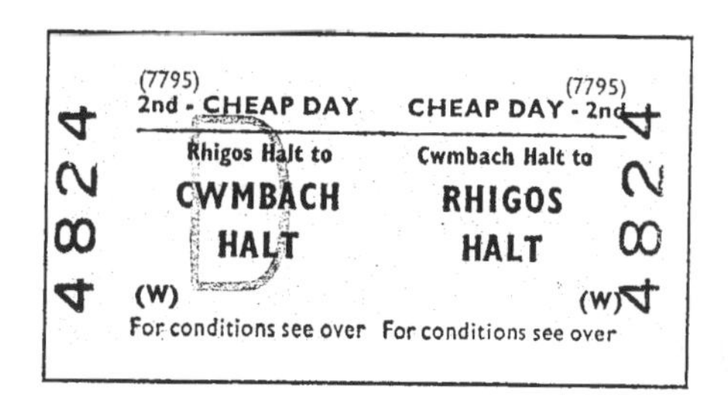

13. The southern part of the footbridge was retained and a new alignment was positioned under it. The old trackbed is on the left as no. 37272 approaches the new river bridge on 3rd April 1984. (P.Jones)

14. No. 37894 is seen from the footbridge as it hauls empties for Tower Colliery near Hirwaun on 3rd April 1992.The VoNR exchange sidings with the Aberdare Canal had been north of this site in the first years of the line. The bridge had come from Wheatley, on the closed Princes Risborough - Oxford line. (R.H.Marrows)

ABERDARE HIGH LEVEL

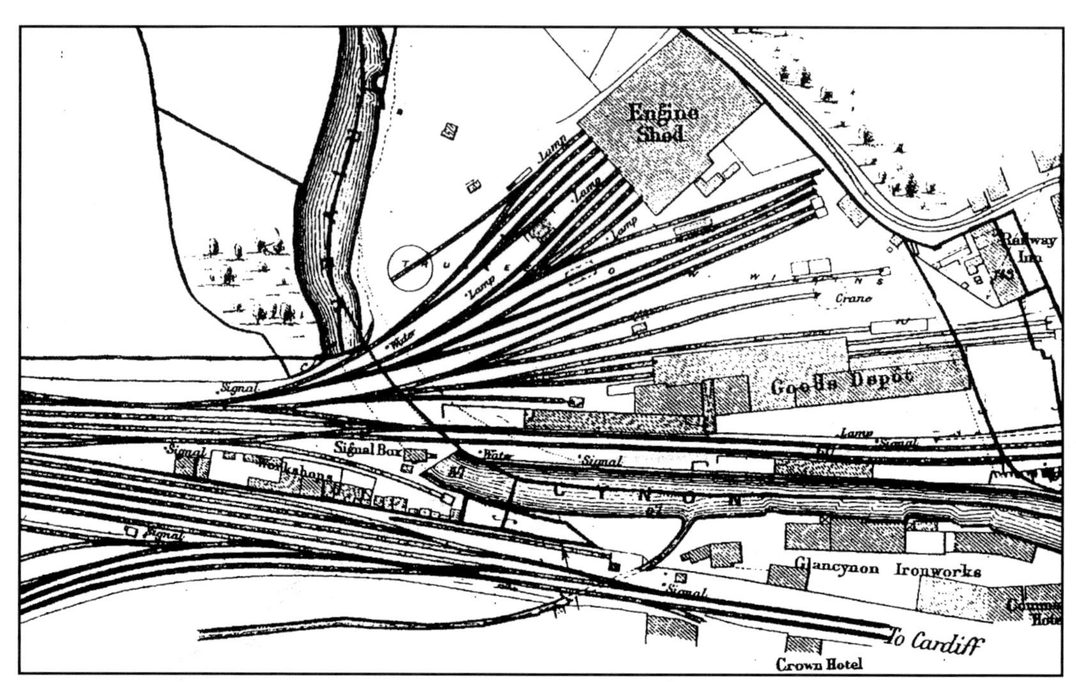

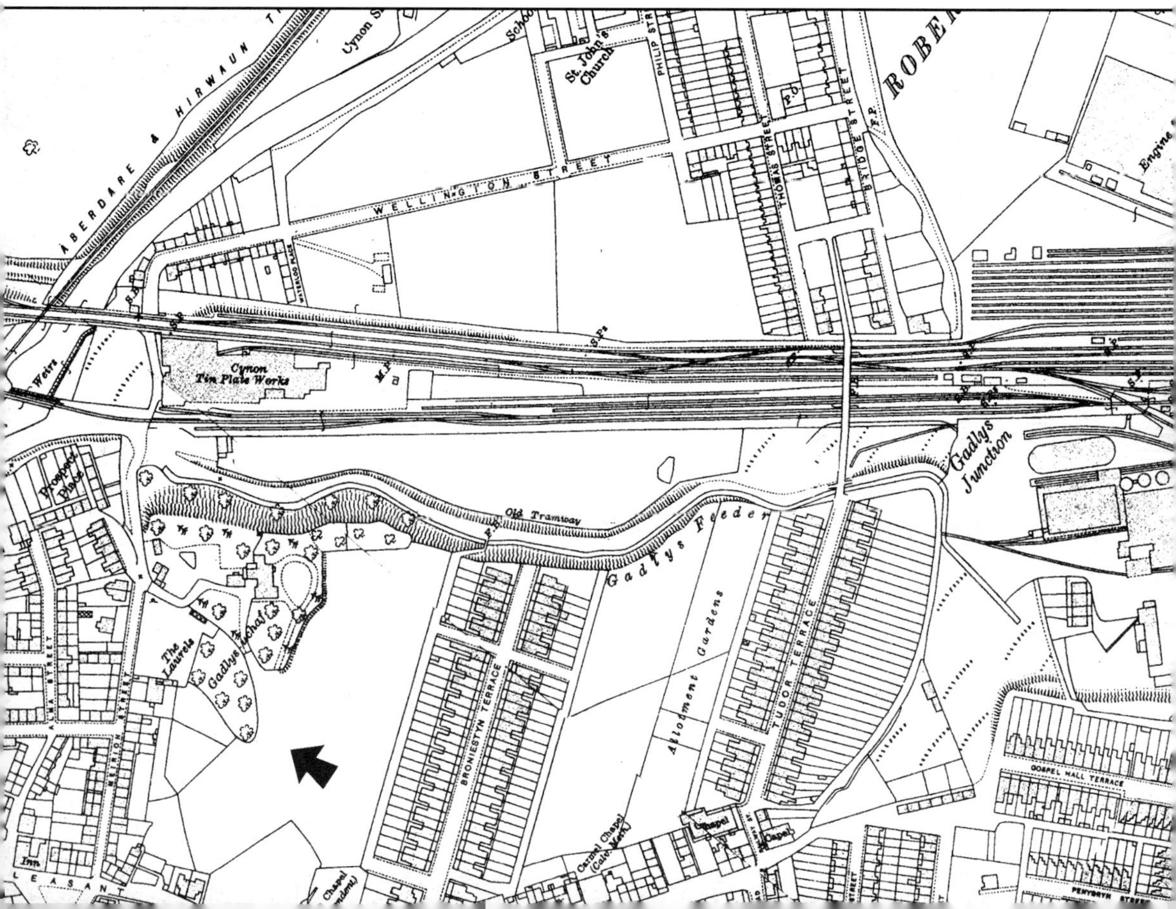

←

VI. An official plan from around 1900 reveals the second location of the engine shed. Half of it had been erected in 1867 and a further four roads followed in 1872. Closure came in 1908 with the opening of the new shed shown on the map below. The crane (right) was rated at ten tons; the turntable was 45ft long and there was an allocation of 49 engines here in 1901.

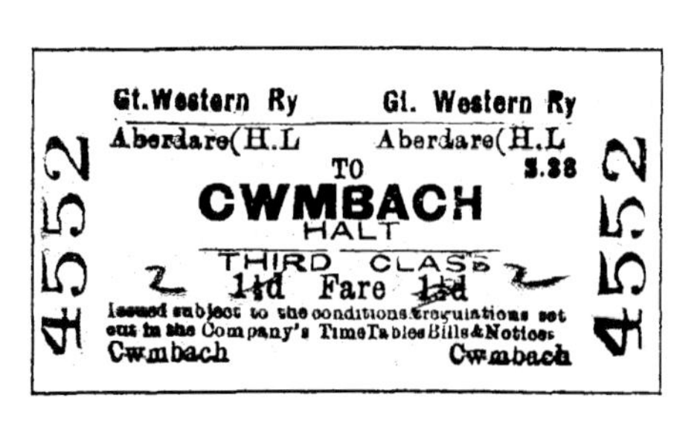

VII. Our route is top right on this 1919 survey and the TVR is below. The 1908 GWR engine shed spans both pages, while the TVR joins the GWR at Gadlys Junction on the left page. Three signal boxes are marked, but only two were in use. The one on the right of the left page was Dare Junction. The brickworks and curved sidings spanning the pages closed in 1936. They were on the site of Gadlys Ironworks, which also had many sidings. The power station and tram depot are nearby; below them is the curve of the 1866 Dare Valley Railway. This became part of the TVR in 1889 and closed in 1959.

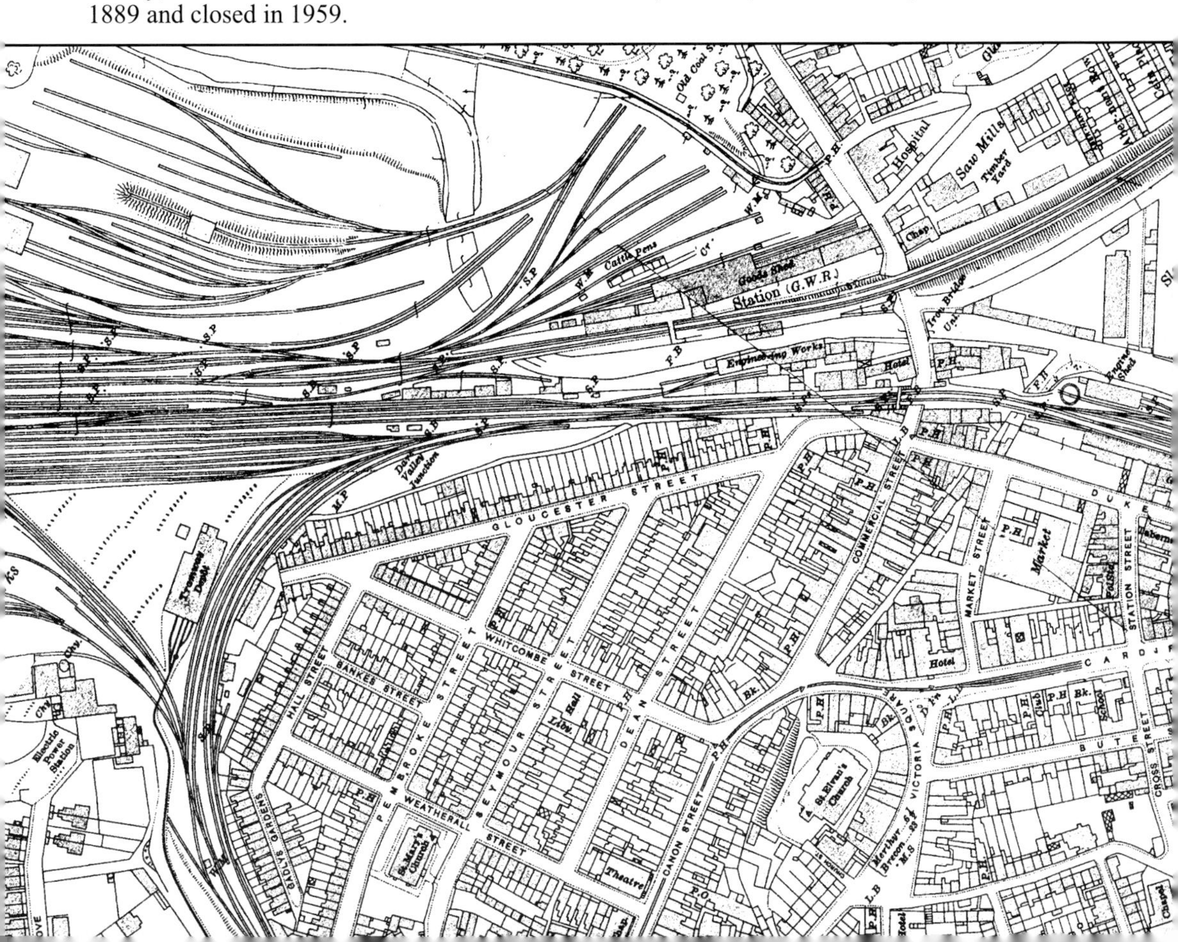

15. This southward panorama is from before 1907, when the signal box on the right closed. The siding behind it served an exchange line with the TVR, via two gates; a direct link was provided here in 1927. The building in the centre was the original engine shed, but its doorways were moved off centre after the broad gauge tracks were abandoned. Behind it is the roof of the first station, a terminus. On the left is the water tank, which was adjacent to the 1907 engine shed. (RCT Libraries)

16. This view in the other direction is prior to 1924, when "High Level" was added. The 1851 building on the right was as specified by I.K.Brunel, engineer to the VoNR, for use as a terminus. A single line platform in the foreground was added in 1864, when passenger services were extended to Mountain Ash and beyond. (M.J.Stretton coll.)

17. Staggered platforms were provided when the route was doubled in 1872, owing to the proximity of the river on the right and the approach road on the other side. The previous building can be seen in picture 15. The train is bound for Neath in about 1961. (W.A.Camwell/SLS)

18. No. 6149 was working in the other direction on the same day and was recorded on the barrow crossing. The entrance to the station is on the right. (W.A.Camwell/SLS)

19. The down platform is viewed from the station approach road, across the site of the broad gauge platform. Good shelter was required from the prevailing wind. (H.C.Casserley)

20. The connection to the Low Level station is shown in detail in March 1963. It was signalled for reversible running, but was not used regularly for passenger trains. Note its steep descent to the former TVR lines. (E.Wilmshurst)

21. Passengers had to make their way along the road busy with parcels vans serving the shed on the right. This photograph is from 27th July 1963 and includes the belfry, complete with its bell. Few such relics then remained anywhere in Britain. (P.J.Garland/R.S.Carpenter coll.)

22. Moments later, the photographer turned to record the down platform and the summit at the far end of it. Beyond the bridge over Commercial Street, the line drops sharply at 1 in 65. (P.J.Garland/R.S.Carpenter coll.)

23. No. 4169 leaves the carriage sidings in July 1963 and passes the shunters cabin. The 1907 signal box had 54 levers and was originally known as Aberdare Yard. It closed as Aberdare High Level Yard on 22nd August 1965, but wagon load traffic here continued into the 1980s. (P.Chancellor coll.)

24. The signal box is in the distance, beyond the stays supporting the stout fence forming a windbreak for the up platform. Unusually, the latter has railings at one end, plus a quaint step for staff to avoid the gates. (Stations UK)

25. This was the 10.6pm from Aberdare on the last day, 13th June 1964. There had been no regular diesel passenger trains. The staff numbered 127 in 1938 and cost £23,576 that year. (G.Davis/B.King coll.)

26. The route was single line southwards from 15th June 1964 and it was taken out of use on 4th July 1971 only to be reopened on 29th July 1973, for reasons explained in caption V. (G.Davis/B.King coll.)

27. Soon after closure, the down platform lost its canopy and the waiting room its roof. This picture emphasises the space constraints at the site and includes the second pedestrian entrance. Part of Glancynon Ironworks is on the left. (G.Davis/B.King coll.)

28. Only the railings of picture 24 remained obvious on 20th October 1979, as the "Deep Duffryn Diddler" railtour called for photographs. The front of the train is on the 1 in 97 gradient down from the bridge. The next three photographs were taken on the same day. (D.H.Mitchell)

29. Less obvious in earlier views is the 1925 building, but removal of its associated canopy made photography easier. The foreground is the trackbed of the TVR connection, which had been removed in 1973. (D.H.Mitchell)

30. A panorama in the other direction from almost the same viewpoint shows the commencement of double track, which is far from parallel. The lines on the left had served Robertstown opencast site until January 1975. (D.H.Mitchell)

31. Crossing the river and the running lines, we look back at the remains of the terminus (centre), which was used as four warehouses, but was destroyed by fire on 7th November 1982. Two were injured and a 14-year old was charged with arson. (D.H.Mitchell)

32. A new platform surface and a ticket office were provided on the site recorded in picture 22 and they came into use on 3rd October 1988, with one train every two hours. This is the 15.21 to Barry Island on 1st August 1995, formed of two "Pacer" railbuses. (N.W.Sprinks)

33. Hertfordshire Railtours employed nos 33109 and 33116 to haul their "Faulty Tower" excursion on 2nd October 1995, by which time restoration of the 1925 structure as offices was nearing completion. It is in the background of the next picture. (R.H.Marrows)

34. When photographed on 23rd March 2006, the yard had been cleared of all but one siding; this was close to the former up platform. An additional access path to the platform had recently been provided, it being behind the camera. The service interval was by that time 30 minutes. (V.Mitchell)

ABERDARE ENGINE SHED

←

35. This panorama of the engine shed and factory dates from 1951 and is from the south. The low building with tall chimneys housed the sand driers. (D.K.Jones coll.)

Aberdare	1903	1913	1923	1933
Passenger tickets issued	180894	516944	397220	84574
Season tickets issued	*	*	670	362
Parcels forwarded	58631	84207	49232	28872
General goods forwarded (tons)	3198	14107	12771	2395
Coal and coke received (tons)	8111	6758	15689	10815
Other minerals received (tons)	13511	22440	14993	2393
General goods received (tons)	22396	40329	94909	34289
Trucks of livestock handled	758	793	813	271

(* not available.)

←

36. The turntable at the centre of all operations was photographed on 13th July 1958. In 1954, there were 56 locomotives allocated here. (H.C.Casserley)

37. On shed on 7th August 1958 were nos 8464 and 48761 (right), together with no. 9712 near the incline for coal wagons. (G.Adams/M.J.Stretton coll.)

38. The shed was recorded from a passing train on 6th June 1963, by which time it was in terminal decline, but the breakdown train was still present (left). The Western Region shed code was 86J. (R.H.Marrows)

→

39. No. D9511 is arriving on 19th December 1964 and was still in pristine condition. To maintain this, it was stabled in the repair shop, along with no. D3428. (R.H.Marrows)

→

40. Nos 5256, 3699 and 4278 were recorded in the shadow of the water tank on 1st September 1964. All steam ceased and the shed closed on 1st March 1965. (M.J.Stretton)

Z 60
D 9511
3796

NORTH OF ABERDARE

41. The engine shed is in the background, as no. 3655 shunts at Gadlys Junction in 1959. Photographs 41-43 were taken from the footbridge shown on the left page of map VI. The point rods lead to the signal box, which closed on 15th June 1964. It had 41 levers. (P.Jones)

→

42. Robertstown Crossing signal box is in the background of this and the next picture. On the right is the 1941 siding for British Earthmoving Machinery Ltd, which became Hayes Plant Ltd in 1946. The siding closed in 1966. (G.Davis/B.King coll.)

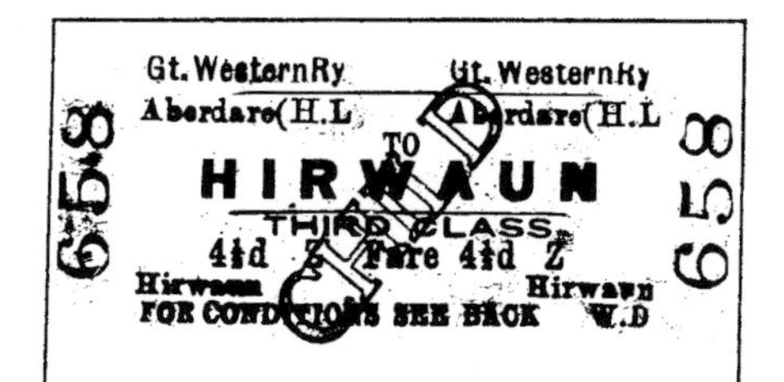

→

43. The sidings served Robertstown opencast site and marked the northern limit of the TVR in this valley. The land to the right of them was the site of the Cynon Tin Plate Works - see map VI again. It had sidings from both railways. The TVR had a platform here called Mill Street, until 1912. (G.Davis/B.King coll.)

44. The 21-lever Robertstown signal box was in use until 1st February 1987, latterly as a ground frame. The gates were replaced by full lifting barriers in November 1976. The line was singled northwards on 2nd October 1967. (G.Davis/B.King coll.)

45. The other end of the box is seen on 15th January 1985, as two Hastings units roar up the incline while working the "Cymru DEMU". There had been a siding on the left of the camera for Ysguborwen Colliery in 1908-20 and for Aberdare Cables in 1937-78. (P.Jones)

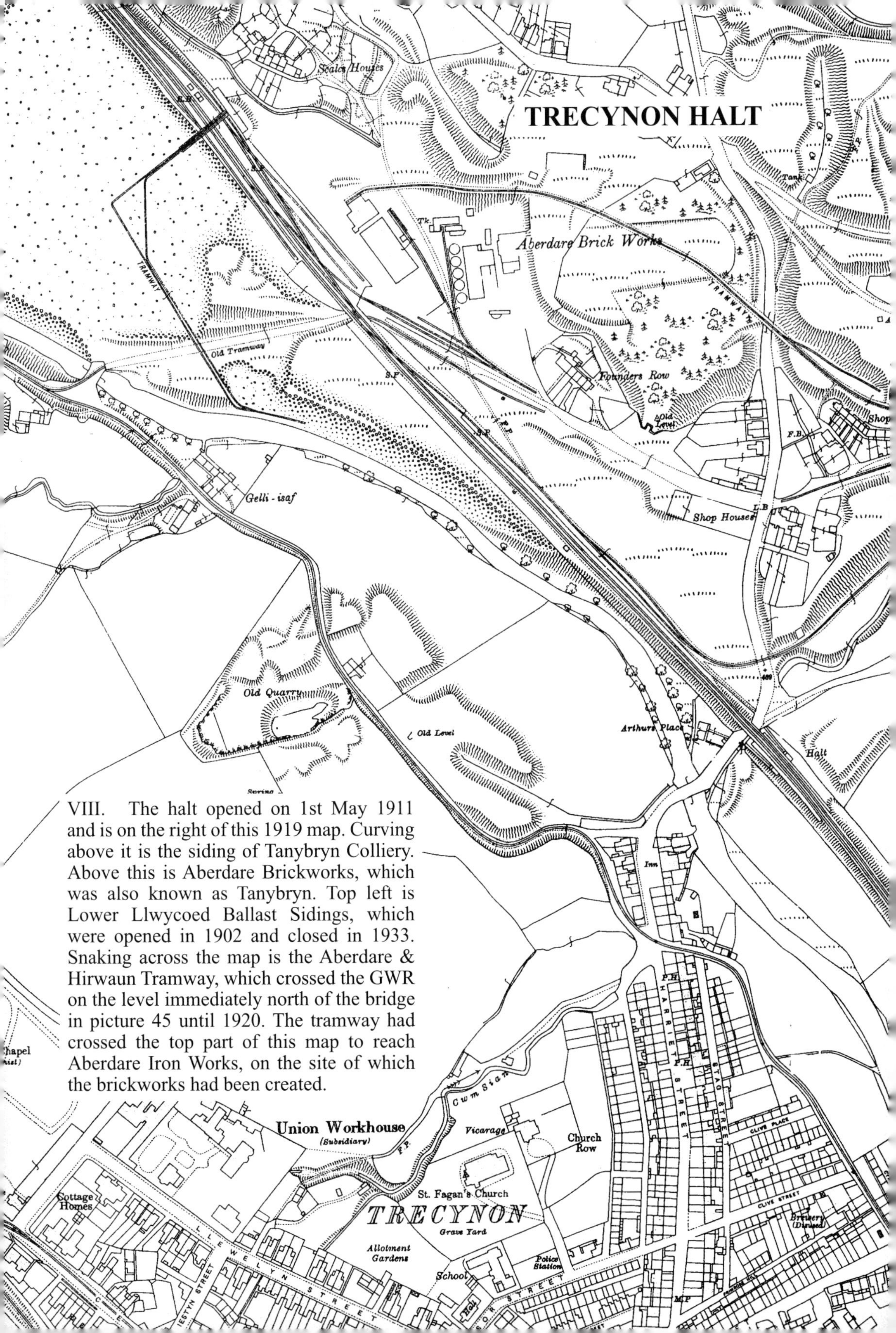

VIII. The halt opened on 1st May 1911 and is on the right of this 1919 map. Curving above it is the siding of Tanybryn Colliery. Above this is Aberdare Brickworks, which was also known as Tanybryn. Top left is Lower Llwycoed Ballast Sidings, which were opened in 1902 and closed in 1933. Snaking across the map is the Aberdare & Hirwaun Tramway, which crossed the GWR on the level immediately north of the bridge in picture 45 until 1920. The tramway had crossed the top part of this map to reach Aberdare Iron Works, on the site of which the brickworks had been created.

46. The line was on a gradient of 1 in 49 in the vicinity of the halt, which changed little in its 53 year life. The loco is class 8F 2-8-0 no. 48420. (G.Davis/B.King coll.)

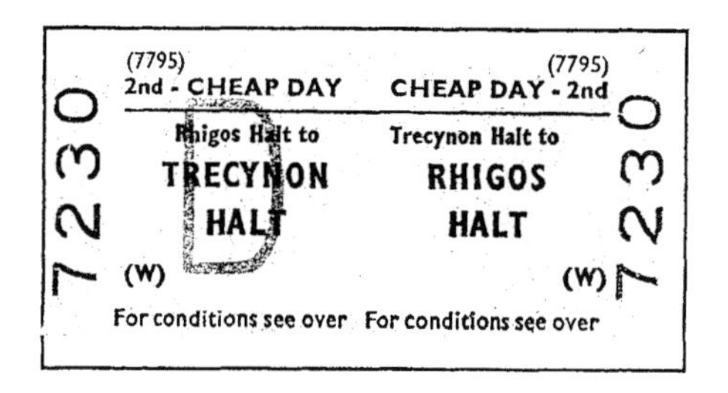

7230	7230
(7795) 2nd - CHEAP DAY	(7795) CHEAP DAY - 2nd
Rhigos Halt to	Trecynon Halt to
TRECYNON HALT	RHIGOS HALT
(W)	(W)
For conditions see over	For conditions see over

GELLI TARW JUNCTION

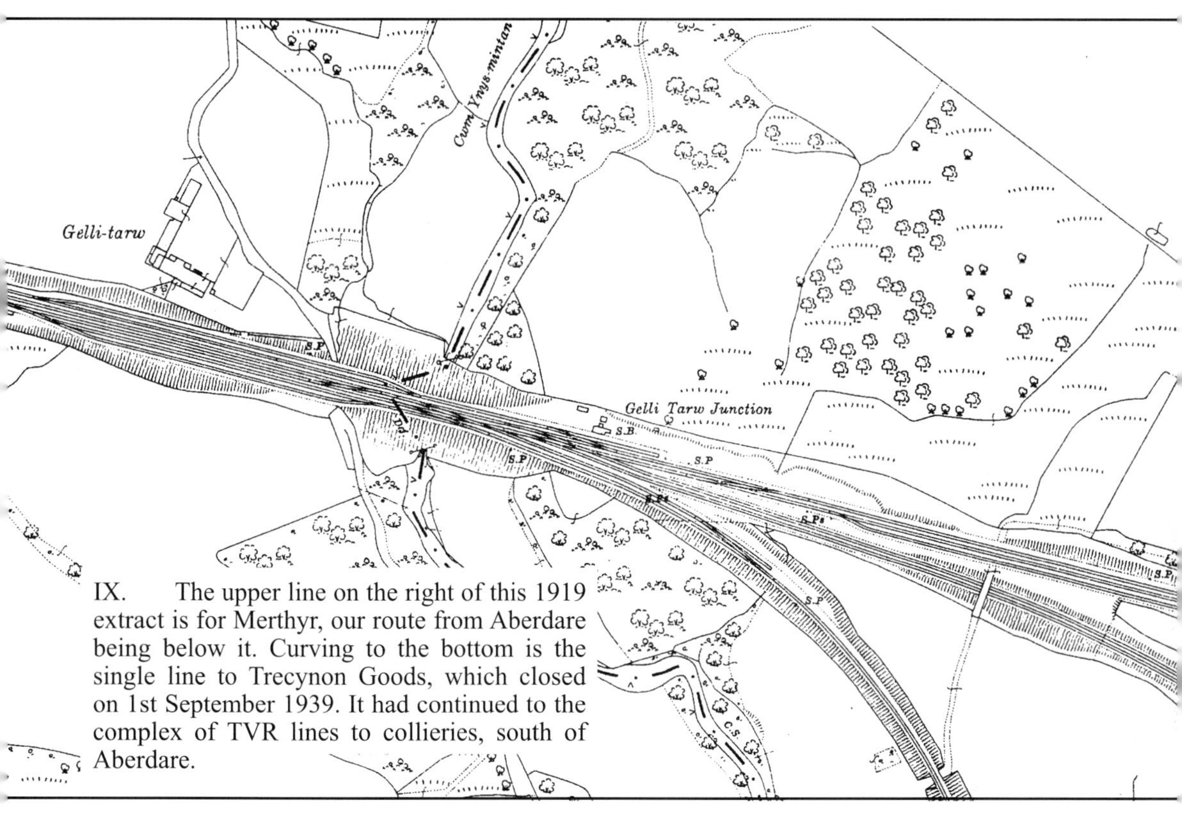

IX. The upper line on the right of this 1919 extract is for Merthyr, our route from Aberdare being below it. Curving to the bottom is the single line to Trecynon Goods, which closed on 1st September 1939. It had continued to the complex of TVR lines to collieries, south of Aberdare.

47. This view from April 1964 has the shiny rails of the Aberdare route curving right, the stub of the Trecynon Goods line on the extreme right and the single line to Merthyr going straight into the distance. This closed completely on 31st December 1962 and the 59-lever signal box followed on 2nd October 1967. (R.H.Marrows)

Merthyr Branch

LLWYDCOED

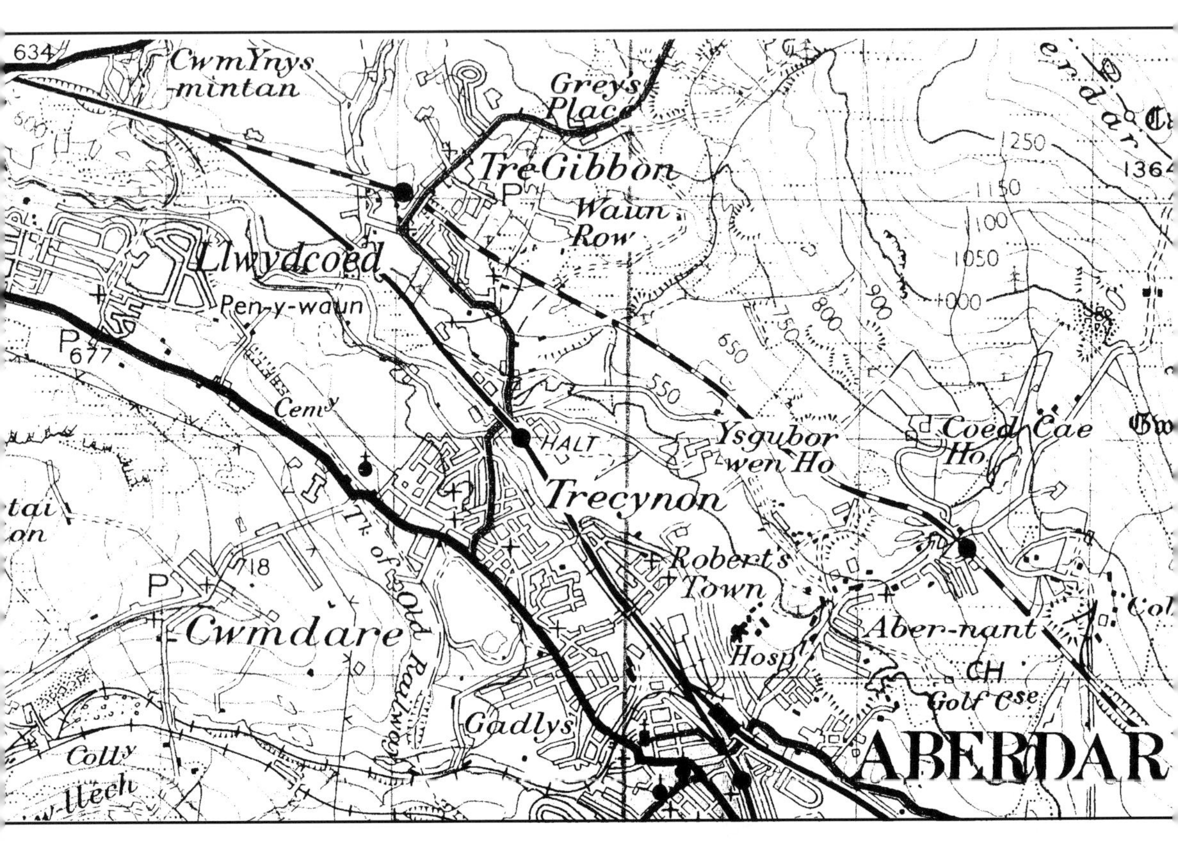

X. The hatched line from the top left to the lower right is the western part of the branch, the tunnel mouth being in the lower right corner. Before the tunnel was completed, there was a temporary station top left, called Merthyr Road. The map is at 2ins to 1 mile and is from 1954.

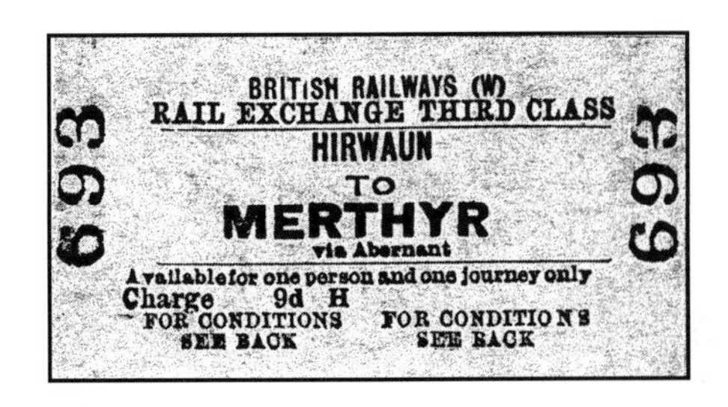

48. The station had no sidings and was in use throughout the life of the line. Its location is in the centre of the map. (G.Davies/RCT Libraries)

49. Residents of the area were well provided with rail transport as Trecynon Halt was within easy walking distance. (C.Nethell/RCT Libraries)

ABERNANT

50. Unlike Llwydcoed, the platform was on the south side of the line, but like it, there was no goods siding. Passenger traffic was generally light, except on special occasions that justified a photograph such as this. (RCT Libraries)

51. Paraffin lamps had been replaced by gas by the time that this photograph was taken prior to the removal of the signal box and signals in 1931. The coach is being propelled towards Merthyr. Note the inclination of the trees due to the prevailing wind. The building still exists. (RCT Libraries)

52. A 1951 picture features another autotrain bound for Merthyr and the station name in the grass. There were lines northward to Blaennant Colliery from 1900 to 1929 and further east there was a connection to Werfa Colliery until 1954; its shaft was in use from 1845 to 1908. Tunnel Pit siding was near the tunnel mouth and was in use from 1900 to about 1918. (RCT Libraries)

MERTHYR

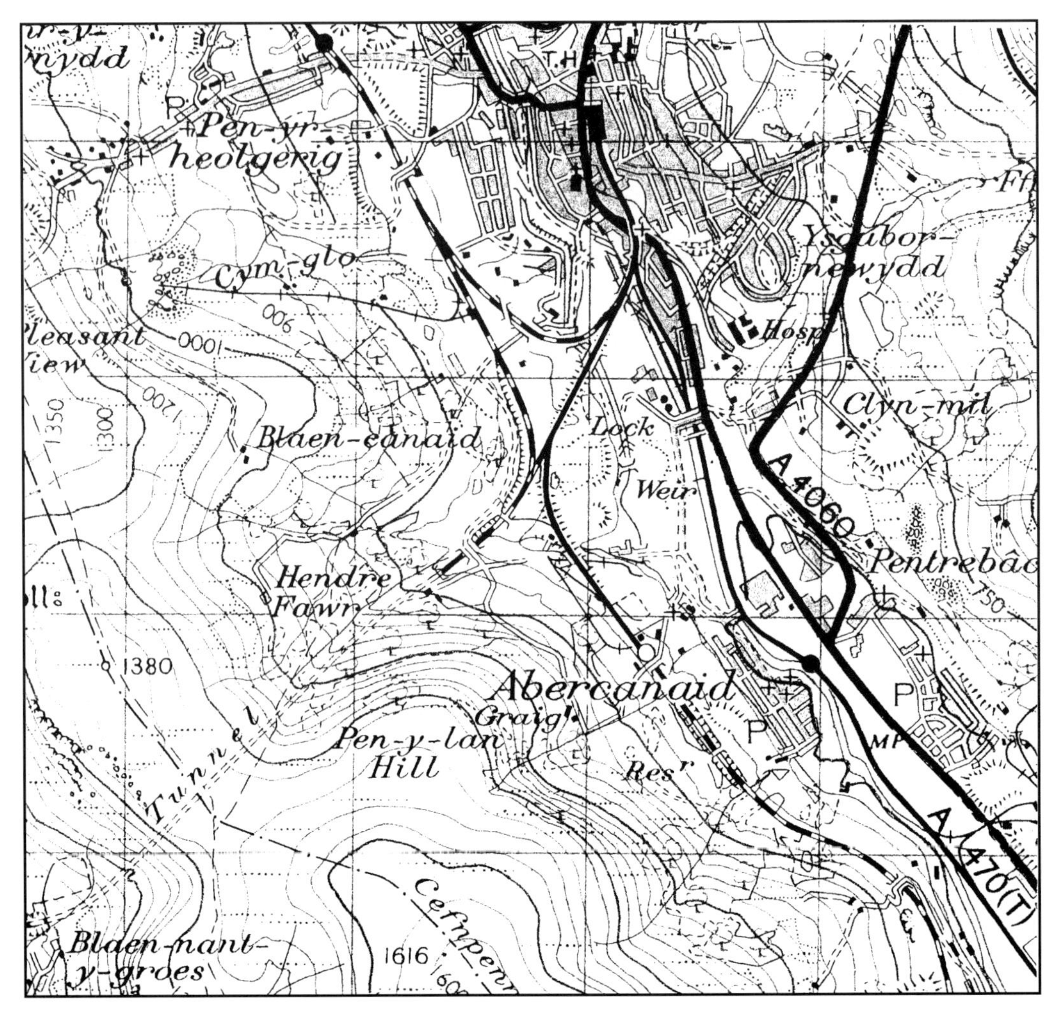

XI. Merthyr Tunnel was 1 mile 375yds in length and is lower left on this 1954 extract at 2ins to 1 mile. Upper left is the route featured in the *Abergavenny to Merthyr* album; it was completed to Merthyr in 1879. The first passenger service to the town was provided by the TVR (lower right, solid line) in 1841. The parallel single line was GWR and Rhymney Railway Joint, it opening in 1886.

53. A 1951 panorama includes all five platforms. The TVR had its own terminus at Plymouth Street until 1877. The station shown was opened on 2nd November 1853. (H.C.Casserley)

54. The engine shed and coal stage were photographed on 6th May 1951. The shed was built in 1877 and extended in 1932. Numbered 88D by BR, it had been home to 20 locos in 1947. (H.C.Casserley)

55. The overall roof had reached the end of its life and was replaced by this canopy before this photograph was taken in 1961. The crew take a rest before returning with no. 6433 to Hirwaun. (D.K.Jones coll.)

56. The rear of the Hirwaun train (right) was recorded on the same day. Alongside is a DMU about to take the TVR route to Cardiff. With only this line now in use, there is only one platform; it has been 200yds south of these since 14th January 1996. (D.K.Jones coll.)

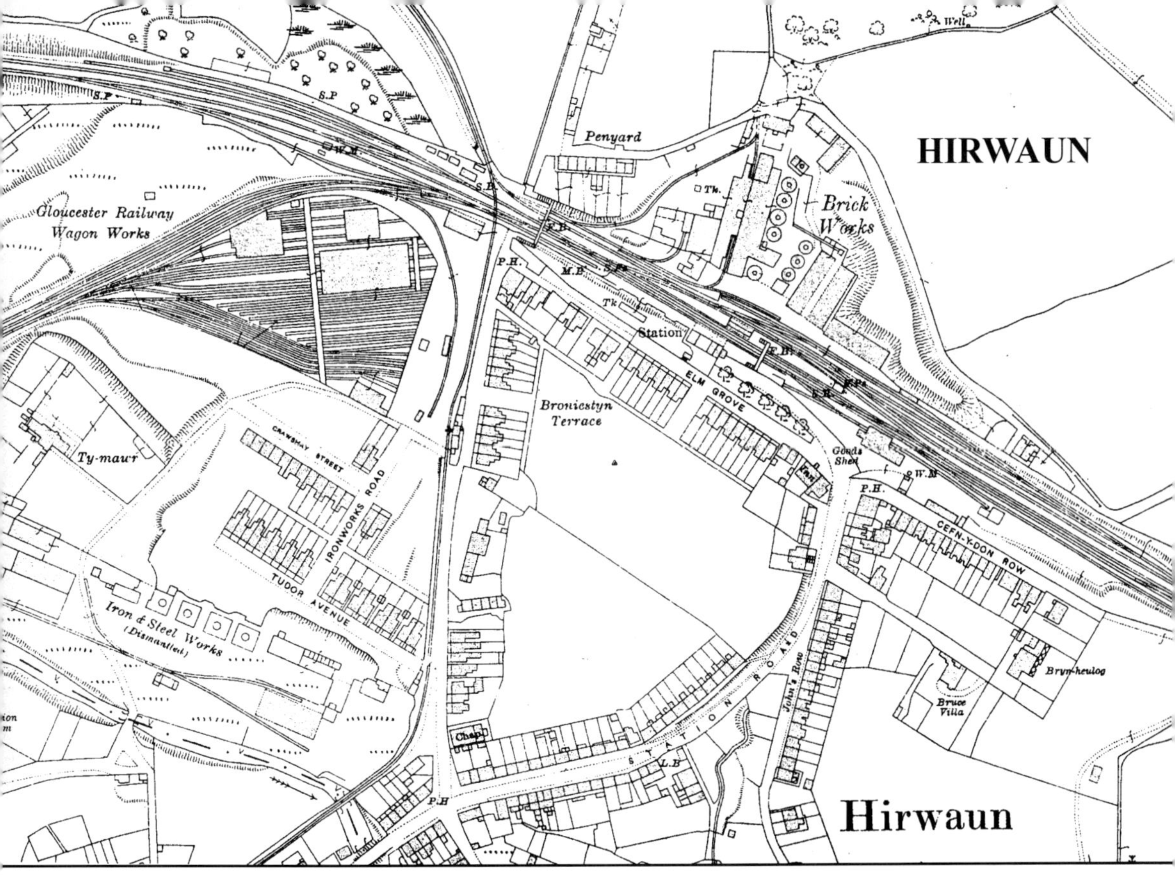

XII. The 1920 edition has the Aberdare and Hirwaun Tramway vertically. The flat crossing of the main line was taken out that year and the line northwards to Penderyn Quarry was connected to the GWR, as shown.

57. An eastward view has the island platform for branch trains on the left and a wagon of gas cylinders for carriage lighting on the right. The spelling was Hirwain until 1928, it meaning "Long Heath"; pronunciation is usually "here-wine". (RCT Libraries)

58. The staff numbered 40 in 1923, but this postcard was probably produced earlier than that. This is a view towards Neath. (RCT Libraries)

59. A train from Neath, hauled by 0-6-0PT no. 9792, waits for water filling to be completed, while a Merthyr train stands on the right. (W.A.Camwell/SLS)

Hirwaun	1903	1913	1923	1933
Passenger tickets issued	75689	119699	110867	45000
Season tickets issued	*	*	493	84
Parcels forwarded	4213	5768	5121	10581
General goods forwarded (tons)	931	972	1540	422
Coal and coke received (tons)	5153	11125	32655	2842
Other minerals received (tons)	5008	30188	5552	1647
General goods received (tons)	3933	10298	11013	5613
Trucks of livestock handled	82	128	90	51

(* not available.)

60. The Merthyr autotrain will have arrived at the platform in the foreground and is crossing to the loop line on 11th April 1955. (H.C.Casserley)

61. Taken a few minutes later, this photograph includes a view through the goods shed. It contained a 30cwt crane. The structure beyond the branch train had been part of the brickworks, but was then owned by South Wales Refractories Ltd. (H.C.Casserley)

62. During a tour of Wales on 9th July 1953, the Queen left her train at Newport and rejoined it here. It continued to Swansea behind two "Castle" class 4-6-0s, reversing at Neath. (RCT Libraries)

63. No. 4668 (left) is working the 5.35pm Swansea to Pontypool Road on 18th August 1962. Most such trains only stopped twice north of Ncath. The 6.50pm to Merthyr is headed by 0-6-2T no. 5626. (M.Dart)

64. The Merthyr service did not use the loop if there was no connection to makc, as witnessed here with no. 6433 at the rear of the train. This applied at 7.20am and 5.54pm, in the final years. (D.Johnson/Millbrook House)

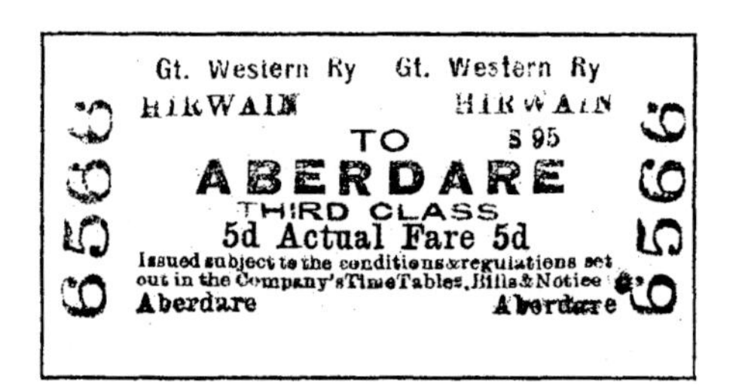

65. The route to Aberdare received most through trains after 1864 and it was doubled in 1872. The goods yard closed on 4th May 1964, nine years after this photo had been taken. (P.J.Garland/R.S.Carpenter coll.)

66. This panorama gives us a final overview of this once important junction, weeks before its closure. The branch closed at the end of 1962, but the island platform building had gone before that. The goods shed was partially demolished in 1961. (R.H.Marrows)

67. No. D6600 (later no. 37300) runs east in September 1967 and passes the 59-lever signal box, formerly termed "West" and closed on 2nd October 1967. East Box had been in use at the east end of the island platform until 14th June 1953; its frame had 25 levers. (P.Jones)

68. A westward view in 1974 has the running line in the foreground and the private siding to the Penderyn Quarry of ARC Ltd in the distance. The line on the right continued behind the camera to three exchange sidings. (D.K.Jones coll.)

69. Looking west from the footbridge on 30th September 1978, we see no. 37279 with empty limestone hoppers. The line to Penderyn Quarry is on the right. (P.Jones)

70. ARC's Rolls Royce diesel engined loco was recorded on their two-mile long line in September 1979. It closed in about 1986 and stone was subsequently taken by road for loading near Tower Colliery. (P.Jones)

71. The building centre background has been seen in picture 66 and the other end of the line on the left is in the background of no. 69. No. 37796 is hauling empties from Aberthaw Power Station for filling at Tower Colliery on 23rd April 1992. (R.H.Marrows)

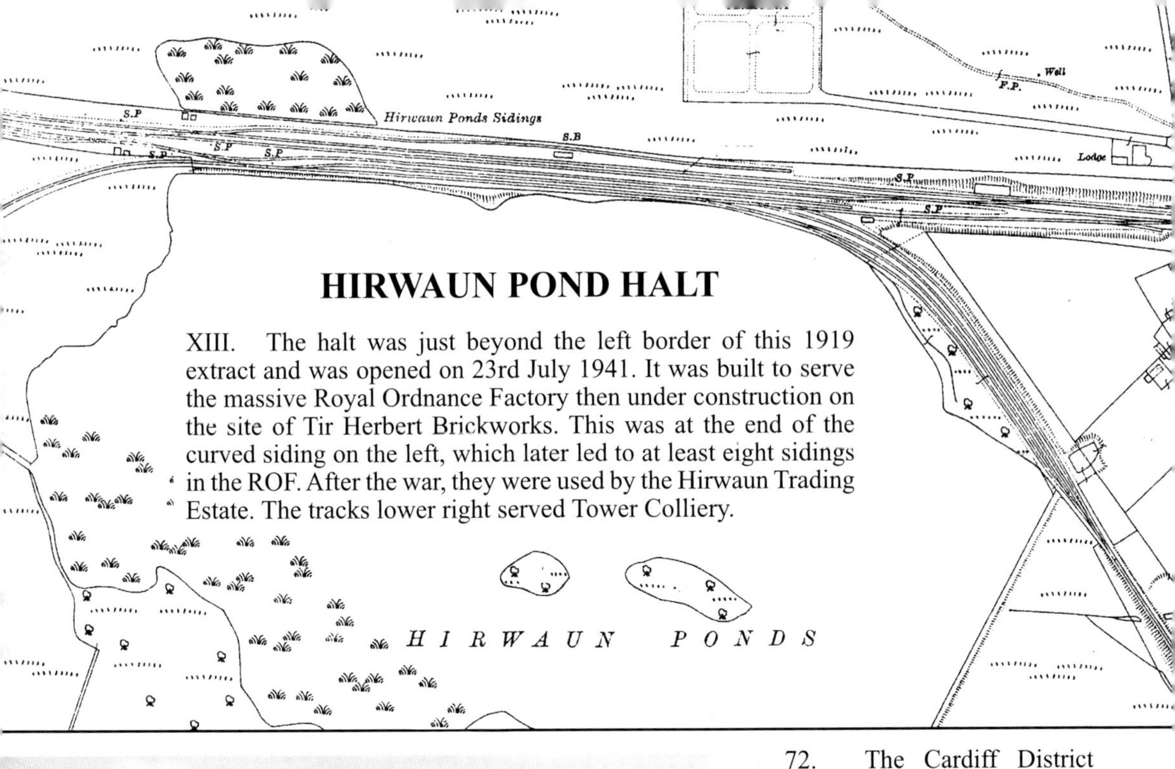

HIRWAUN POND HALT

XIII. The halt was just beyond the left border of this 1919 extract and was opened on 23rd July 1941. It was built to serve the massive Royal Ordnance Factory then under construction on the site of Tir Herbert Brickworks. This was at the end of the curved siding on the left, which later led to at least eight sidings in the ROF. After the war, they were used by the Hirwaun Trading Estate. The tracks lower right served Tower Colliery.

72. The Cardiff District Engineer's inspection saloon was recorded behind ex-TVR 0-6-2T no. 364 in December 1956. To the left of it is the up line; it is on one of the two down running lines in this vicinity. The signal box had 40 levers and was in use from at least 1898 until 2nd October 1967, when the route was singled eastwards and closed westwards. (P.Q.Treloar)

73. The halt was for workers and did not appear in public timetables. It closed in the early 1950s for a period prior to the development of the trading estate. No. 4169 is bound for Neath and has just passed Tower Colliery, which is in the background. Workers trains ran into the estate for a short time.
(G.Davis/B.King coll.)

TOWER COLLIERY

74. A drift was started in 1864 and it was named after Crawshay's Tower, a nearby folly built in 1848. A shaft was completed in 1943 and another drift in 1958. Underground links were made with Mardy Colliery in 1964 and 1986, this becoming the last to raise coal in the Rhondda, in 1990. British Coal closed the entire complex on 22nd April 1994, but an employee buyout resulted in it reopening on 3rd January 1995, under the name of Goitre Tower Anthracite. (R.H.Marrows coll.)

75. No. 37803 is at the loading pad on 9th April 1992, which was built at the end of the single track, and not at a siding. Note that part of a pond remains. Cawood's containers (left) were destined for Seaforth (Liverpool) with coal for export. There were normally two trains each working day in 2005 from here, mostly to Aberthaw Power Station. (R.H.Marrows)

RHIGOS HALT

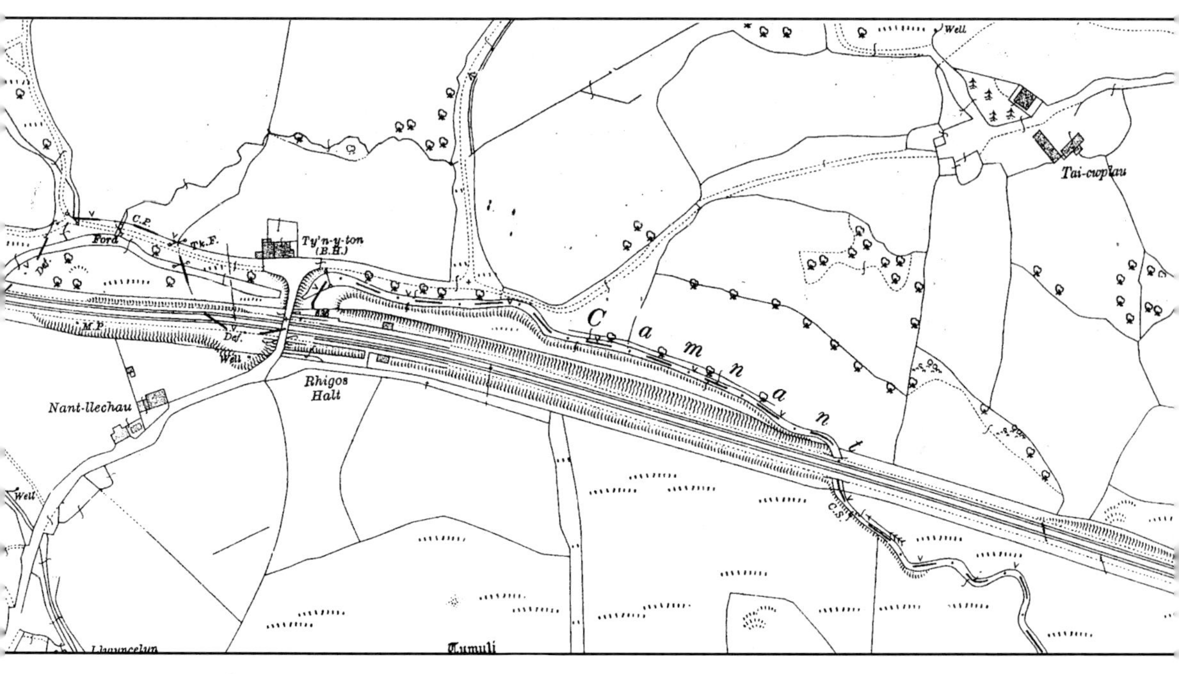

XIV. The halt opened on 1st May 1911, but served only a small and scattered community.

76. The summit of the route was at Hirwaun Pond and Rhigos Halt was built on the 1 in 80 descent to the tunnel. (M.Dart coll.)

77. Three carriage sidings were laid beyond the bridge and they came into use on 17th October 1943, along with the associated signal box, which had 22 levers. A workers service was provided between here and Merthyr for some years. (J.L.Berry/RCT Libraries)

78. The signal for the carriage sidings is the one on the right. The enlarged shelter for wartime munition workers is evident, as a train departs east on 2nd May 1961. The sidings and box were in place until 1965. (Stations UK)

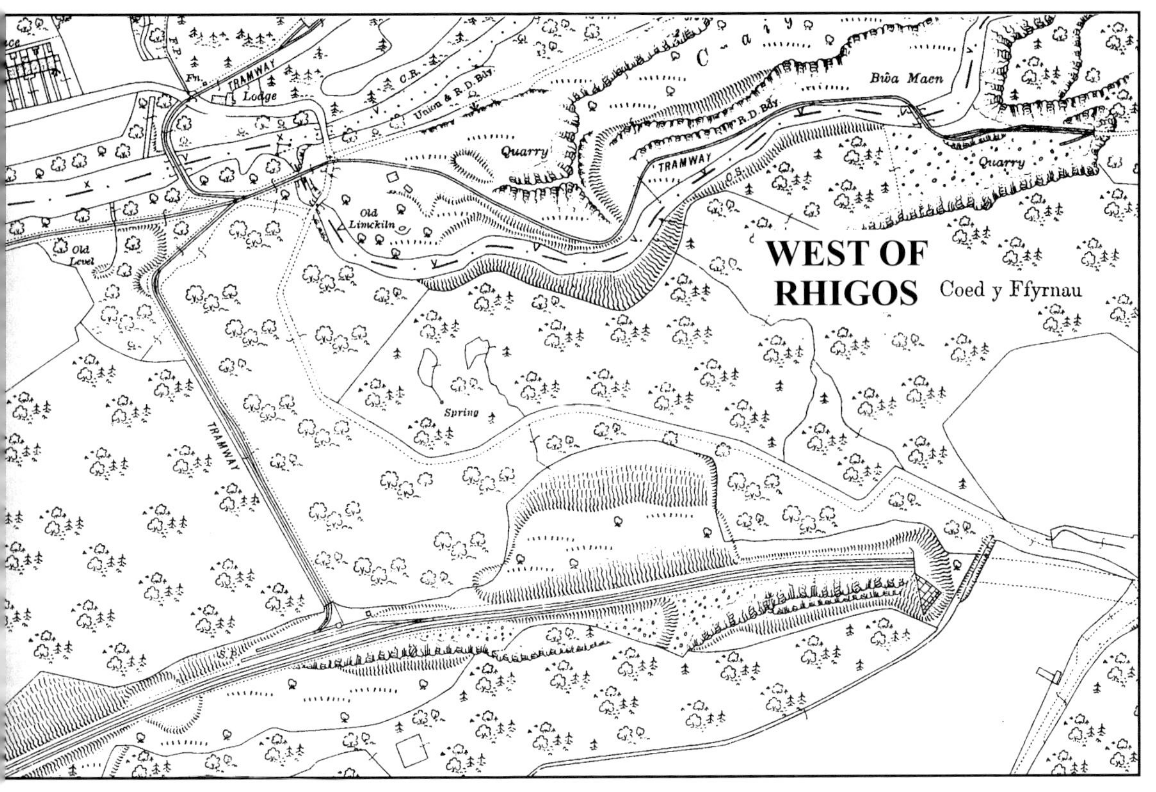

XV. On the right of this 1919 map is Pencaedrain Tunnel, which is 526 yds in length. The siding on the left served the Dinas Rock Brickworks of Curtis & Harvey from 1887 to 1935.

79. Rhigos distant signal is evident as we approach the east end of the tunnel in August 1962. It marks the boundary between the Vale of Neath and the Cynon Valley. (M.Dart)

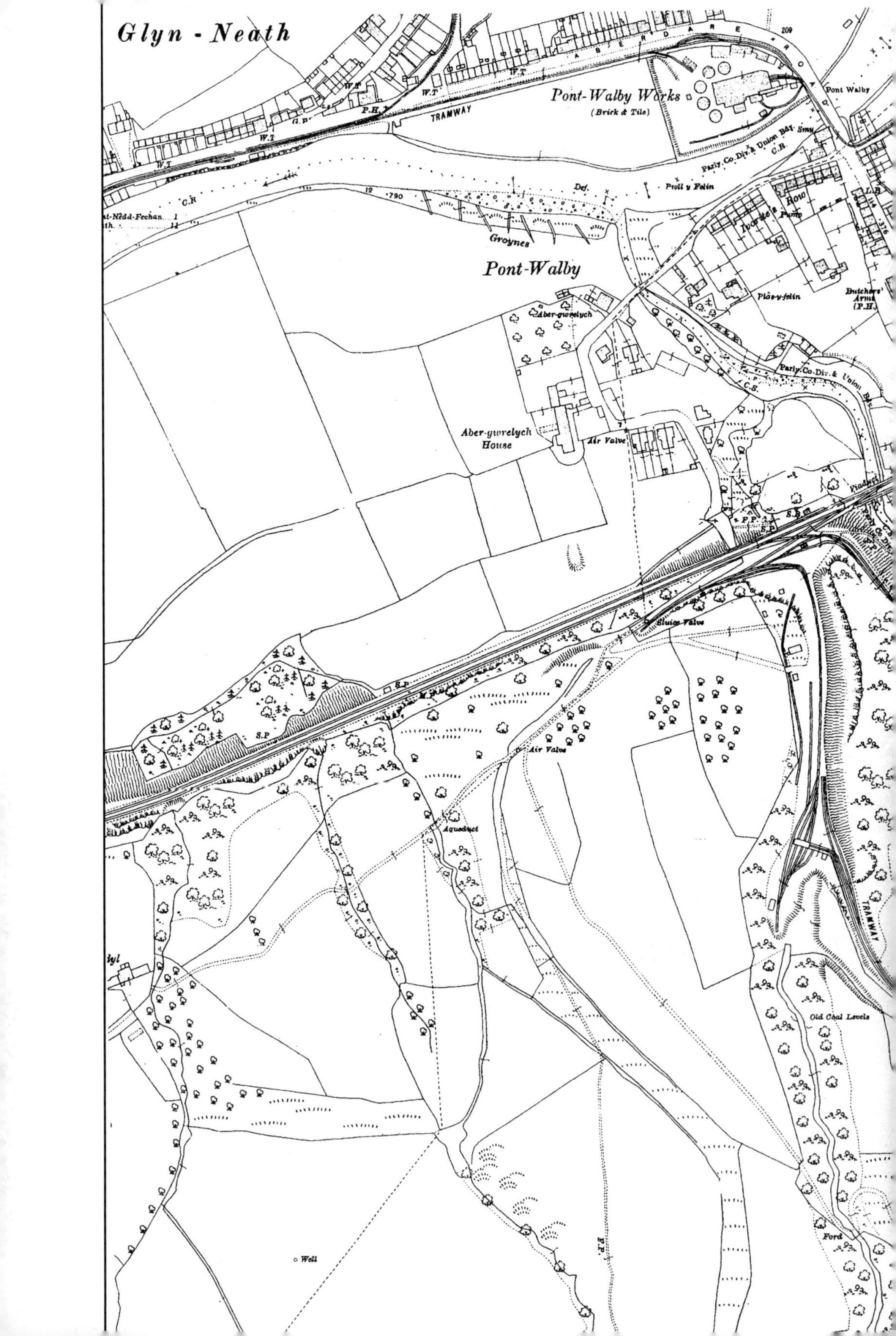

Glyn - Neath
Pont-Walby Works
(Brick & Tile)
TRAMWAY
Pont Walby
Parly. Co. Div. & Union Bdy
Pwll y Felin
Groynes
Pont-Walby
Aber-gwrelych
Aber-gwrelych House
Air Valve
Plâs-y-felin
Butchers' Arms (P.H.)
Sluice Valve
Air Valve
Aqueduct
Old Coal Levels
Ford
Well

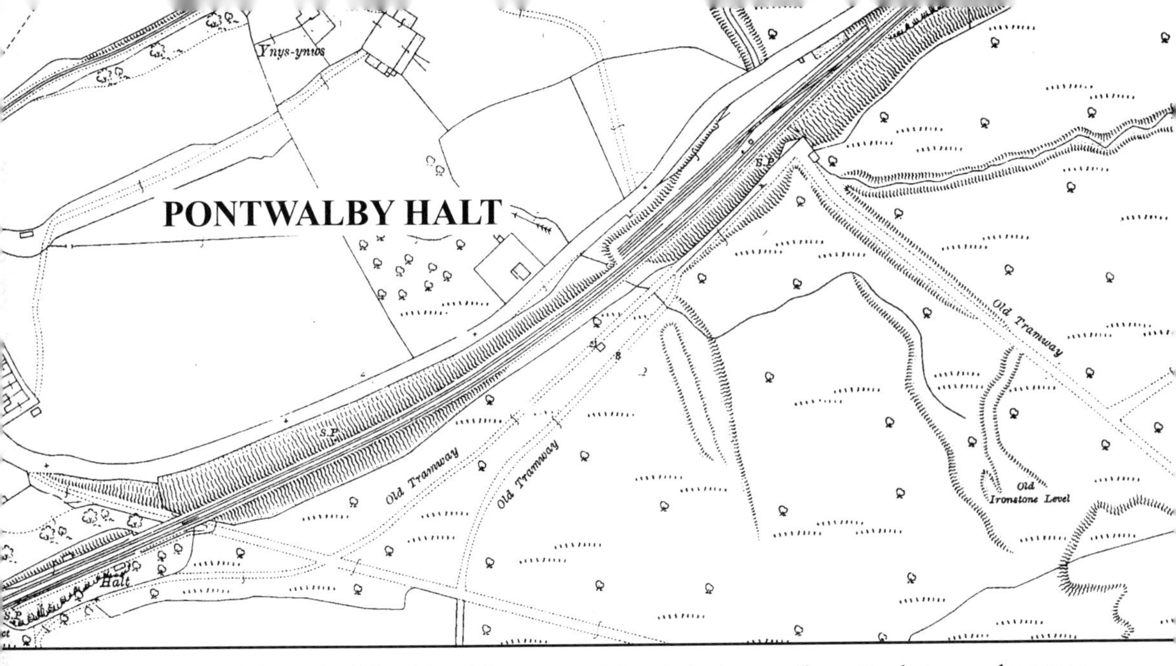

XVI. The halt is on the left of the right page and the viaduct spans the gutter between the pages. Top right are Penrhiw Sidings, which were in use until 1921. On the left page is British Rhondda Colliery. The signal box was renamed Rhigos Colliery in 1943 and was closed on 20th July 1964. At the top is the 1879 Abernant Railway, which was of standard gauge and ran north to serve Rock Colliery. Its No. 2 Drift Mine was in use in 1943-61.

80. The viaduct was a natural subject for a postcard. It had replaced one of Brunel's elegant timber structures and is still standing. (R.H.Marrows)

81. The view east in July 1956 in the rain features little of note, other than track relaying in progress. The halt had opened on 1st May 1911. There was another ¾ mile to the west from 14th January 1935 until about 1945. It was called Cwmrhyd-y-Gau and was for workmen only. (R.M.Casserley)

82. In the other direction, we have the railings of the viaduct between the train and the down starting signal. On the right is the signal box, which had 15 levers. The year is 1961. (Stations UK)

GLYN NEATH

XVII. The 1919 survey shows a line crossing the River Neath and diverging into sidings for the Aberpergwm Colliery. There was one short and one long GWR siding south of the station, the latter being under the words "Cattle Pen". All the others served the Cwmgwrach & Empire Colliery complex. Coal has been mined here for over 300 years, and in 1863 Aberpergwm Drift Mine was opened and this was very successful until 1969. However, by 1975 output was 3000 tons per week and good production figures were being maintained 30 years later.

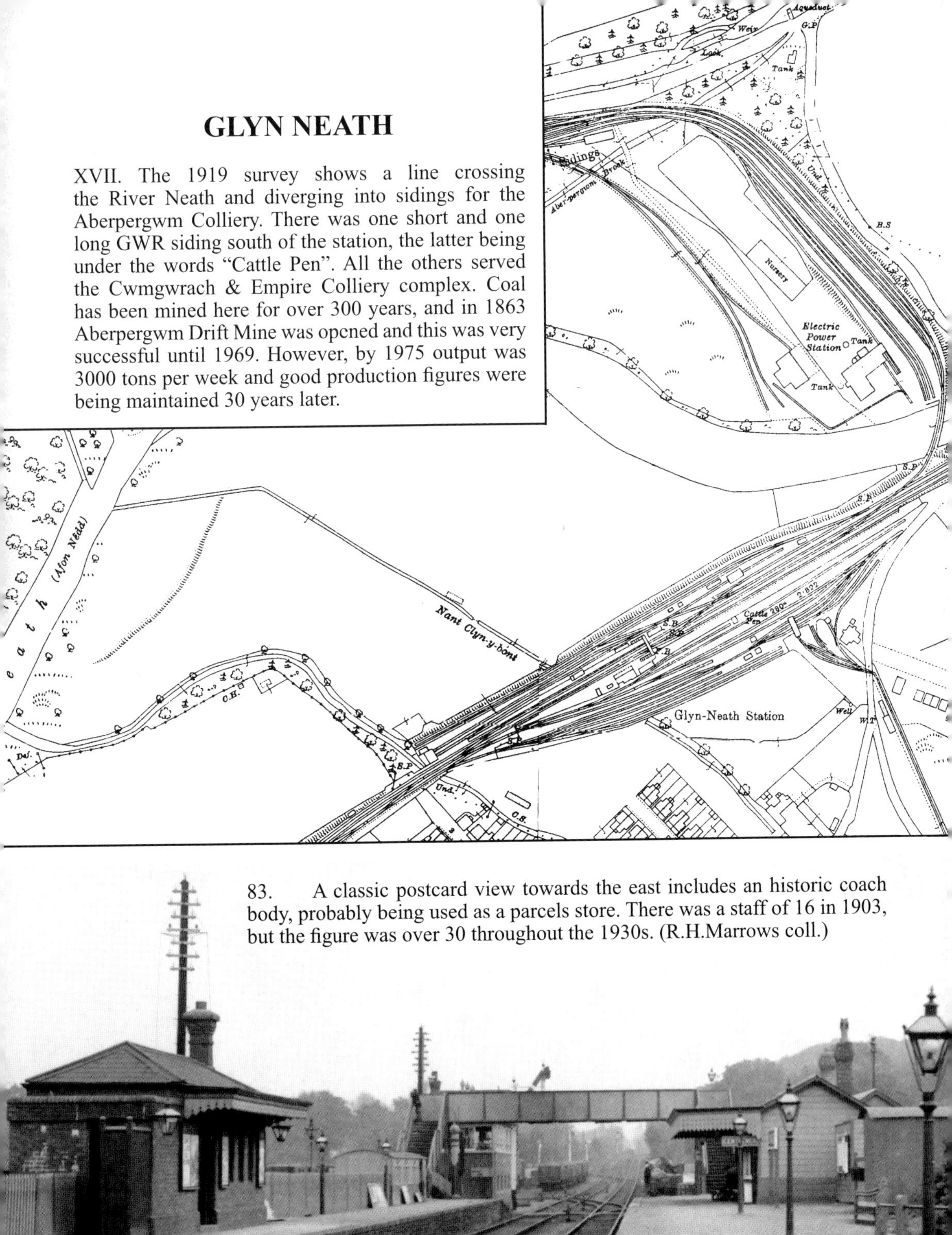

83. A classic postcard view towards the east includes an historic coach body, probably being used as a parcels store. There was a staff of 16 in 1903, but the figure was over 30 throughout the 1930s. (R.H.Marrows coll.)

84. A four-mile climb at around 1 in 50 begins near the signals and so banking engines were kept here from the earliest days. No. 4295 is nearest in this view from the 1950s. (Lens of Sutton coll.)

85. No. 6431 approaches the platform with a short train from Aberdare on 4th April 1959. The signal box had a 38-lever frame and was in use until 13th April 1969. (M.Dart coll.)

→

86. From the same viewpoint on 14th January 1961, we see no. 6818 *Hardwick Grange* waiting for the signal to clear, while working an up freight train. (M.A.N.Johnston)

Glyn Neath	1903	1913	1923	1933
Passenger tickets issued	37014	84134	78550	33461
Season tickets issued	*	*	319	94
Parcels forwarded	6143	17026	16358	19403
General goods forwarded (tons)	632	1408	690	628
Coal and coke received (tons)	3582	2403	1191	576
Other minerals received (tons)	4166	10479	8800	2544
General goods received (tons)	3525	14601	21864	28774
Trucks of livestock handled	12	29	45	10

(* not available.)

87. The down platform received a new building in about 1950, but it is indistinct in this April 1964 view. The bridge seen above the footbridge carried a narrow gauge railway from Aberpergwm Colliery to the NCB plant on the right. The former GWR siding is the unoccupied one. (R.H.Marrows)

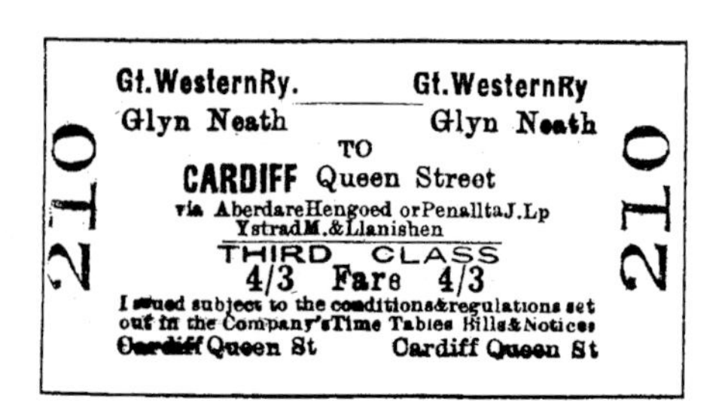

WEST OF GLYN NEATH

88. A siding for Wenallt Colliery was opened ½ mile west of the station in 1924 and the adjacent 24-lever Rheola signal box controlled it until 1956, when it became a ground frame. Mining ceased in 1983, but the siding closed in 1967, by which time the name Blaengwrach Drift Mine was in use and around 4000 tons of coal was produced weekly. This undated poor quality view includes a train bound for Neath passing by. (A.Price/B.King coll.)

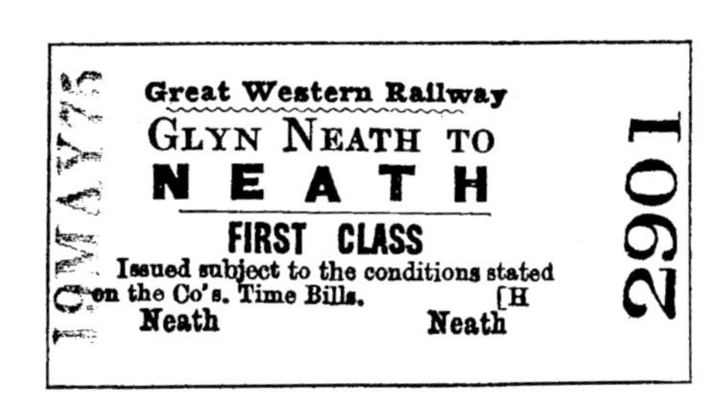

89. Nearly one mile west of the junction for Aberpergwm Colliery was another line to that mine. The branch gave a more direct route and it came into use in March 1926. The loading plant (right) was south of the old A265. The 23-lever Aberpergwm Colliery Junction box was in use from 1924 to 1967. The line to Glyn Neath was not used regularly after 1971. No. 37205 is seen with the last working from the colliery (right), this being on 29th April 1985. (B.King)

90. Half a mile west of the site of the station, a new coal loading pad was opened in March 1994 at Cwmgwrach. Known as Ryans Disposal Point, it received coal from Wenallt, Lyn, Rheola and Pentreclywdau Mines, plus Cwm Nant Lleci Quarry. No. 60010 is about to leave with a loaded train on 28th September 2003. There were three trains per week in April 2005. (D.Llewellyn)

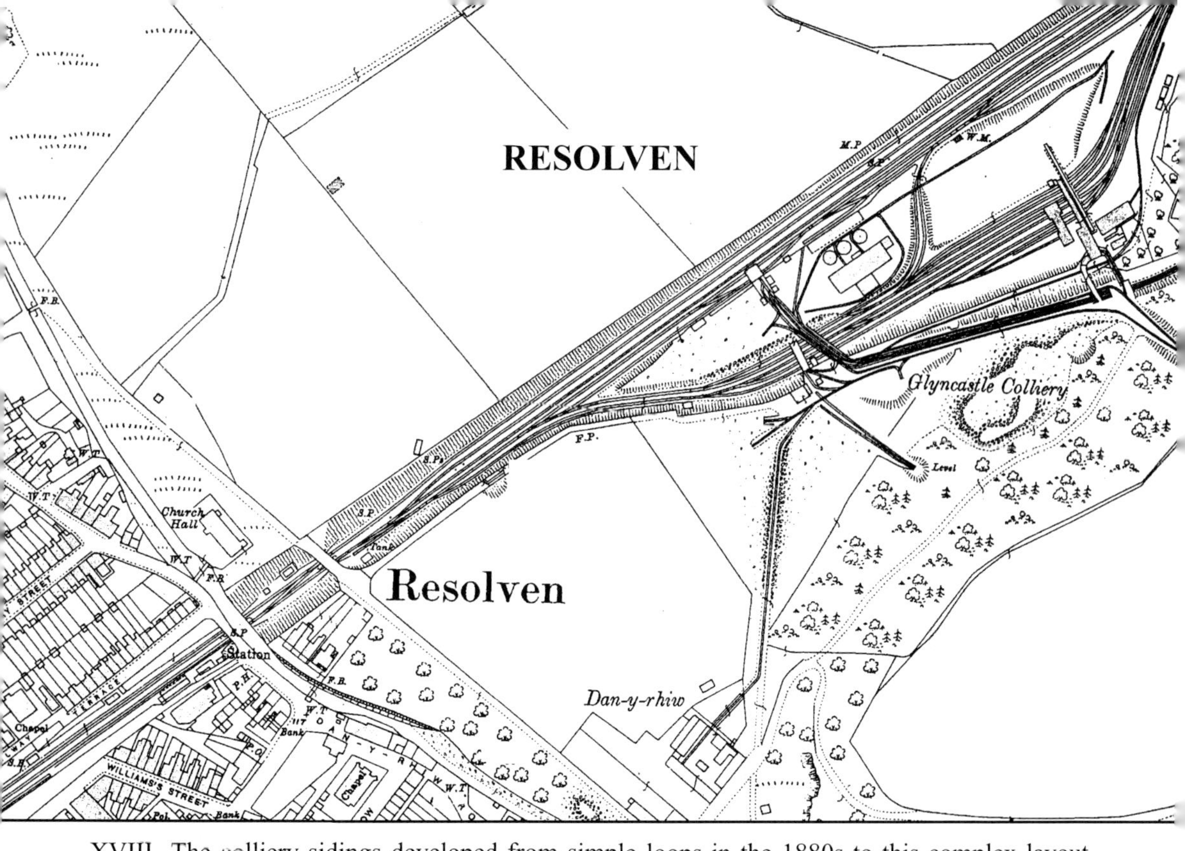

XVIII. The colliery sidings developed from simple loops in the 1880s to this complex layout, which is shown on the 1918 edition.

91. Steam railmotors were introduced to the route in 1905 and the presence of a top hat suggests that this photograph was taken on the first day of service. No. 7 had been completed in May 1904. (Lens of Sutton coll.)

92. Oil lamps were still in use when the bearded station master was recorded with his frock coat and his clerk with a top of the range bicycle, complete with white-walled tyres and chain guard. The population in 1901 was 2389. (M.Dart coll.)

Resolven	1903	1913	1923	1933
Passenger tickets issued	46239	87440	102100	47984
Season tickets issued	*	*	360	67
Parcels forwarded	5501	13402	13497	14711
General goods forwarded (tons)	717	9925	9190	6181
Coal and coke received (tons)	4417	5680	42822	45257
Other minerals received (tons)	6489	14338	13776	9270
General goods received (tons)	2701	9804	8559	6767
Trucks of livestock handled	3	-	2	1

(* not available.)

93. The small Clydach Brook took a short cut to the River Neath on 19th December 1911. The nearest bridge carries both the road and the brook; the map shows three footbridges over the latter. The brick arch is for a private road. (B.King coll.)

94. Although only 100 feet above sea level, snowfall was once frequent. Some of the staff were recorded; there were 11 in 1903, but mostly on two shifts. The figure was 15 to 17 in the 1930s; working hours had decreased and coal traffic had increased. (J.Langford coll.)

95. The colliery and a coal train are included in this postcard view. The water column could be used by locomotives travelling in either direction. Two up lines were created in October 1937, which explains the change of signals in picture 97. (Stations UK)

→

96. A panorama towards Neath includes the single goods siding; its traffic ceased on 21st March 1966. This photograph is from 1961. (Stations UK)

→

97. This is the scene on 11th April 1964 and it features West Box, which had 37 levers and closed on 13th April 1969. East Box was beyond the right border of the map and its 40-lever frame ceased to function on 3rd July 1967. The centre road was taken out of use in October 1966. (R.H.Marrows)

PARCELS &
LEFT LUGGAGE

98. Only the parcels office remains in this view, this traffic continuing until 22nd November 1965, as at Glyn Neath. Just beyond East Box, there had been a down loop from 1937 to 1967 and a siding on the up side for the British Aluminium Rheola Works from 1939 to 1967. (M.Dart coll.)

99. This shot from March 1981 is included to show the access path to the down platform. The route had been singled on 3rd July 1967. (D.K.Jones coll.)

MELYNCOURT HALT

XIX. The halt was opened on 1st June 1905 and it was situated just beyond the lower left corner of this 1919 map. The first siding here was on the down side and served Congreves Brickworks. By 1881, it was used by Lower Resolven Colliery as well, and in 1905 it was added to for New Gored Merthyr Colliery. Permanent closure was in 1928. On the up side, there was a line to Ynisarwed Colliery from at least 1914 until about 1980. It had loaded coal at a loop earlier. Shown on the left is the third signal box; this had 42 levers and lasted until 17th November 1962.

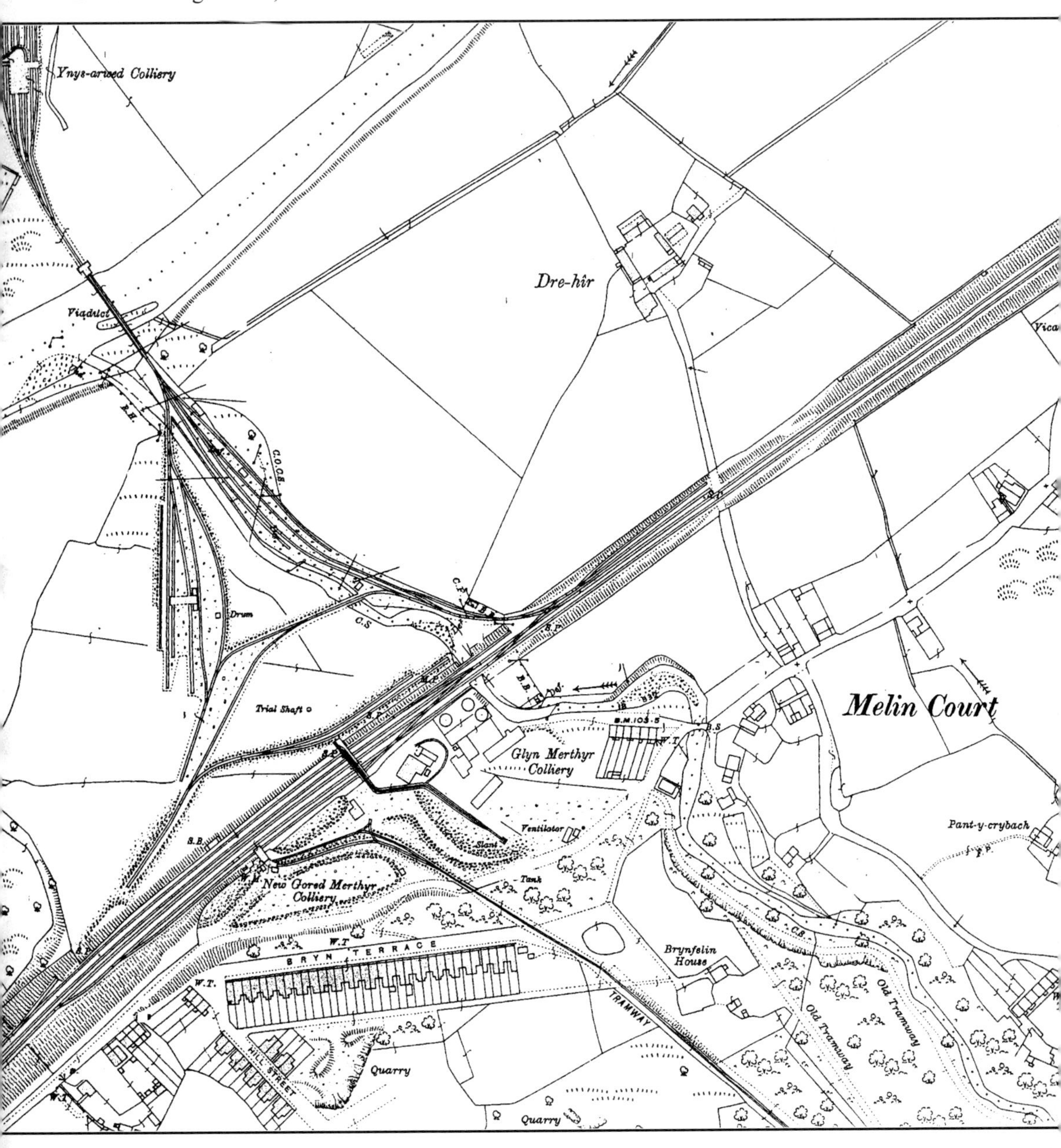

100. The railmotors brought great improvements to local transport. A service to and from Swansea East Dock was operated until 1936. This is a view east soon after the opening of the halt. (Lens of Sutton coll.)

101. Looking in the same direction in 1961, we see bracket signals in the distance. They were for an up loop in the vicinity of the colliery. It had been added in 1913 and closed with the signal box. (Stations UK)

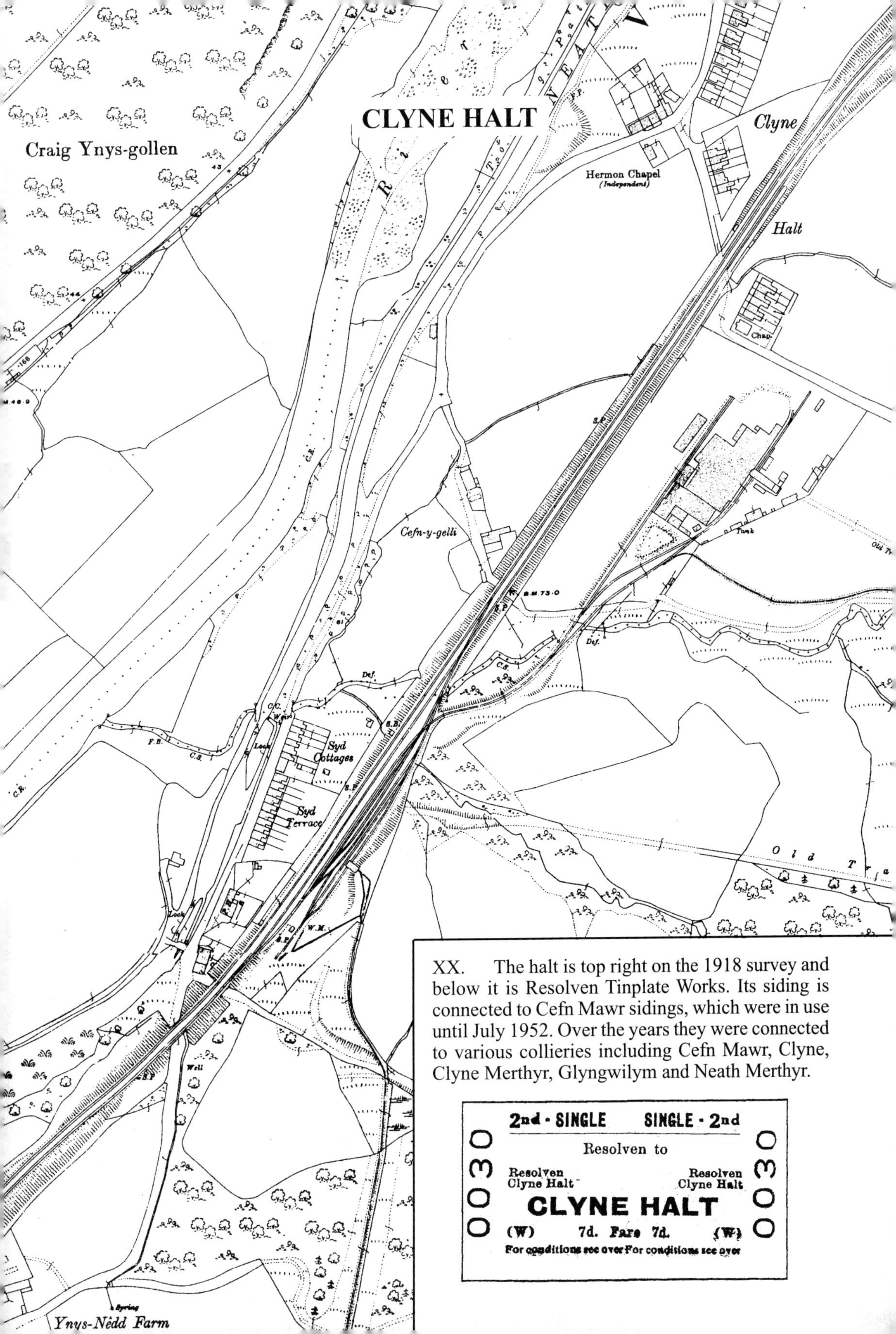

XX. The halt is top right on the 1918 survey and below it is Resolven Tinplate Works. Its siding is connected to Cefn Mawr sidings, which were in use until July 1952. Over the years they were connected to various collieries including Cefn Mawr, Clyne, Clyne Merthyr, Glyngwilym and Neath Merthyr.

102. This northward view up the Vale of Neath has the lock gates on the left (see map) and Cefn Mawr sidings on the right and Clyne Halt in the far distance. One siding had earlier been extended across the foreground, under the main line to a wharf on the river. (B.King coll.)

103. Looking north again, we see the remains of the halt in 1961, clearly little used by that time. Just one lamp post remained. Note that the track spacings were still for broad gauge. Further west, there had been sidings for Wenallt and Neath Merthyr Collieries in the 19th century. (Stations UK)

ABERDYLAIS

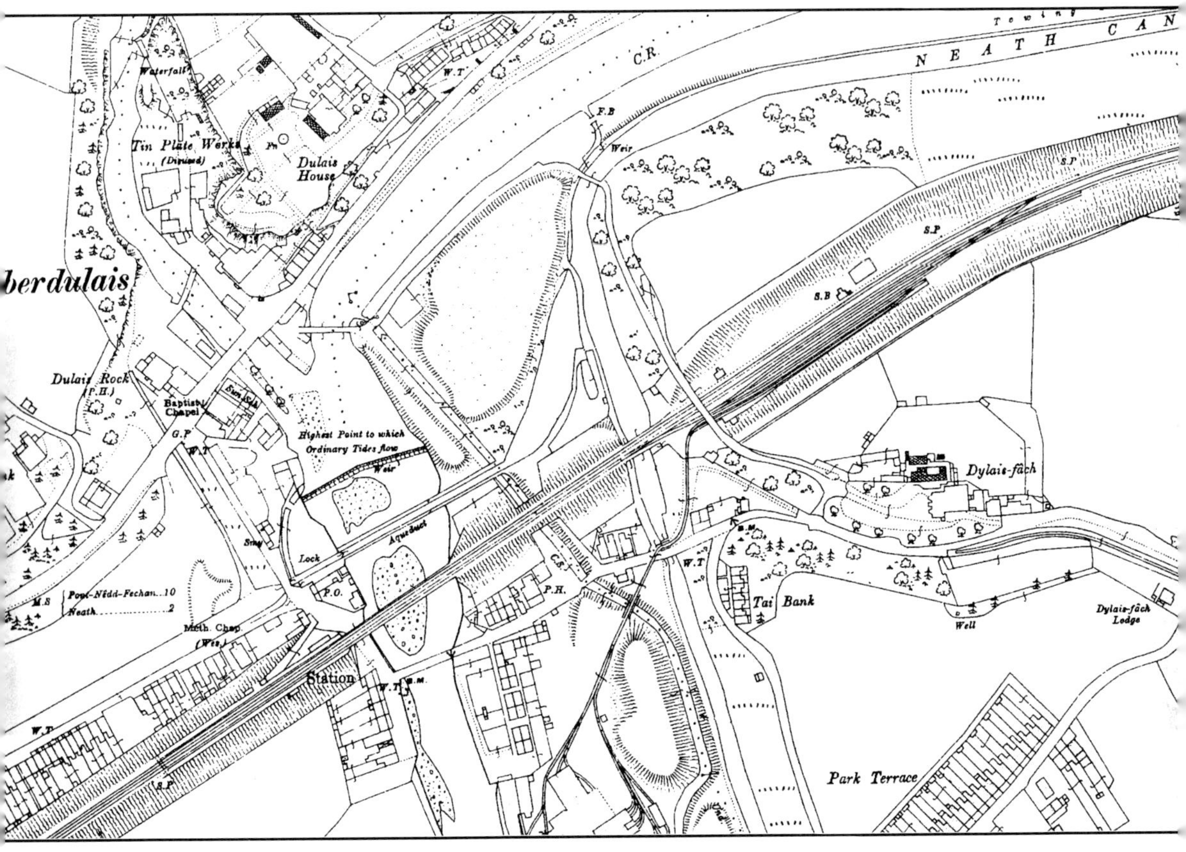

XXI. The 1919 survey has the station on the left and the signal box on the right. The canal bridge is centre. The tinplate works had a private siding from 1890 to 1947 and from it there was a line to Wenallt Colliery for a time. There is evidence of it on the right of the map.

104. A 1956 view towards Clyne includes the parapet of the bridge over the Neath Canal. The siding is in the distance, on the right. There had been a staff of six or seven in the 1930s. (R.M.Casserley)

105. The 2.25pm from Pontypool Road is arriving behind 2-6-2T no. 5102 on 14th July 1959. The station was unstaffed from 7th June 1954 and termed a halt from that time. (R.M.Casserley)

Aberdylais	1903	1913	1923	1933
Passenger tickets issued	31835	75728	114329	15736
Season tickets issued	*	*	167	106
Parcels forwarded	1766	2567	2209	4348
General goods forwarded (tons)	1818	3165	7616	5011
Coal and coke received (tons)	5417	3779	5177	5473
Other minerals received (tons)	8244	3550	9851	7352
General goods received (tons)	757	703	1946	859
Trucks of livestock handled	-	-	-	-

(* not available.)

106. The line crosses the Neath Canal before reaching the overbridge in the distance. The down building had gone by the time that the photographer arrived in 1961. The line was single to Resolven from Neath from 13th November 1966. (Stations UK)

107. In the foreground of this photograph from 13th April 1995 is the 1824 aqueduct for the Tennant Canal over the River Neath. The 73yd long railway viaduct is beyond it and the road bridge is in the background. On the right is the toll house. A pair of class 37s head for Cwmgwrach with a train of empties. (R.H.Marrows)

NEATH
JUNCTION
Vale of Neath
Brewery
Cadoxton House
Neath Junction
Neath & Brecon Junction
Engine Shed
Omnibus Depot
CADOXTON ROAD
DAPHNE ROAD
TENNANT CANAL
Towing Path
GWR
NEATH LOOP
Munl. Boro. Bdy.
High Water Mark of M
RIVER NEATH (Afon Nêdd)
Mud
H.W.M.M.
Allotment Gardens
Allotment Gardens
Corp. Yard
Corporation Yard
Castle Nêdd
R.C. Chap.
Mission Hall
Club
St. Giles's Chapel (Site of)
Station
BRIDGE STREET
ANGEL STREET
CROFT ROAD
JAMES STREET
NEW STREET
THE SQUARE
St. Thomas's Church (Rect.)
Town Hall
Castle Hotel
Hotel
Market
THE PARADE
Bank
ORCHARD STREET
Gwyn Hall
Statue
Warehouse
Hall
St. David's Church
GREEN STREET
QUEEN STREET
Chapel
Engineering Works
Firebrick Works (Disused)
Quay
Aqueduct
ZOAR ROW
BANK SIDE
COMMERCIAL STREET
Chapel
B.Gd.
CATTLE MARKET
CHARLESVILLE PL.
Burial Ground
Indt. Chapel
Town Station
Stone
Shelter
VICTORI

←

XXII. At the top of this 1935 map we have the line from Brecon to the left of the Tennant Canal and our route to the right of it. Nearby is Neath Junction signal box, which closed on 13th November 1966, along with the connection to Neath General, marked as "Town Station" near the lower border. Neath Riverside is on the left, at the end of Bridge Street.

108. The engine shed is top left on the map, but it was rebuilt in 1946, as seen in 1961. Its code was 87A and it was known as N&B shed, its origins dating back to the 1866 Neath & Brecon Railway. (D.K.Jones coll.)

2nd · SINGLE SINGLE · 2nd

756 Glyn Neath to 756

Glyn Neath Glyn Neath

Neath Riverside Neath Riverside

NEATH RIVERSIDE

(W) 1/5 Fare 1/5 (W)

For Conditions see over For Conditions see over

NEATH RIVERSIDE

109. The suffix was "Low Level" in the early years, but was "Bridge Street" from July 1924 to September 1926. Through running southwards by passenger trains ceased on 28th September 1936, but coal continues to Swansea Docks. No. 3611 waits to leave for Brecon on 27th March 1948. (SLS coll.)

110. Both platforms retained their canopies until 1954, when the footbridge was also removed and the up platform taken out of use. (T.J.Edgington)

111. A view north from the sole remaining platform in use on 18th May 1958 includes a train bound for Swansea on the main line, together with Neath & Brecon Junction box. It had been fitted with a new frame with 38 levers in 1957. There had been High Level platforms in 1865-77, to the right of the bridge. The gas in the cylinders was for kitchen car use. (N.C.Simmons)

112. The line on the right of the previous picture served the engineers yard on the left of this one, which was taken after the end of regular passenger service in October 1962. However, there was an afternoon school train departure until June 1964. Access to the building from Bridge Street was at first floor level. (Lens of Sutton coll.)

113. All was destroyed except the up platform and the signal box. Nos 37244 and 37187 have just passed under the main line on 20th September 1979, with coal from Onllwyn, on the former Brecon route. Since 1969, there had been a short single line section beyond the bridge, as far as the junction. (T.Heavyside)

114. The single section was lengthened to a point just south of Bridge Street and the junction signals moved north, beyond the main line. Two class 37s pass under an HST on 11th April 1995, with fuel from Cwmgwrach Colliery for Aberthaw Power Station. (R.H.Marrows)

Other views of this station and the engine shed can be found in our *Brecon to Neath* album.

INTERCITY
43168
894

NORTH OF NEATH GENERAL

115. Reference to map XXII shows that the main line takes a long curve as it crosses the River Neath. We witness an 0-6-2T bound for Swansea on 25th August 1962. (R.Holmes)

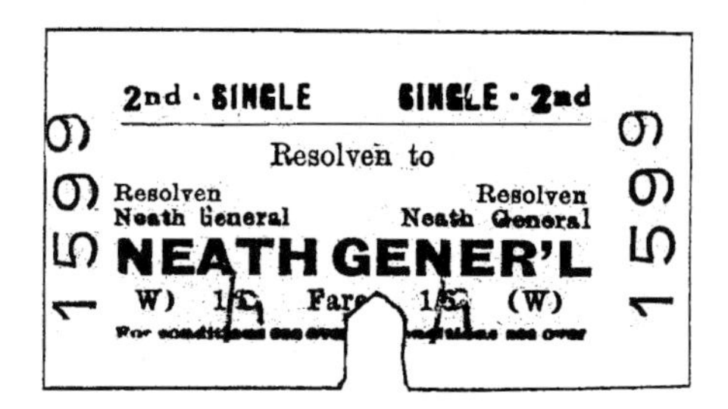

NEATH GENERAL

116. The first station was built near this site in 1850, but closed in 1865 in favour of the High Level one mentioned in caption 111. These buildings date from 1877 and are seen on 9th May 1953, as no. 4522 rests upon arrival with the 8.40am from Pontypool Road. (T.J.Edgington)

117. Providing banking assistance to a Swansea train on 24th May 1959 was 0-6-0PT no. 8442. The train engine is almost over the River Neath, near the site of the second station. (D.K.Jones coll.)

118. Passing the 1929 West Box on 14th January 1961 is BR 4-6-2 no. 70026 *Polar Star*, with a Pembroke Docks to Paddington express, while 0-6-2T no. 6693 waits after arrival from Pontypool Road. (M.A.N.Johnston)

119. After arrival from Pontypool Road at 3.12pm on 20th August 1963, 0-6-2T no. 5647 ran round its train and now stands on the centre road awaiting its return time. (B.S.Jennings)

120. In the right distance is the goods yard, which closed on 22nd November 1965. The engine shed was 1¾ miles beyond it, this closing in June of that year. West Box ceased to function on 8th October 1967. Using the crossover on 11th April 1964 is 0-6-2T no. 6661, while a train from the Vale of Neath line arrives. All was lost, except for parts of the footbridge, during the construction of a new station in 1975-78. (R.H.Marrows)

EVOLVING THE ULTIMATE RAIL ENCYCLOPEDIA

Easebourne Lane, Midhurst, West Sussex.
GU29 9AZ Tel:01730 813169
www.middletonpress.co.uk email:info@middletonpress.co.uk

A-0 906520 B-1 873793 C-1 901706 D-1 904474

OOP Out of Print at time of printing - Please check current availability **BROCHURE AVAILABLE SHOWING NEW TITLES**

A
Abergavenny to Merthyr C 91 5
Aldgate & Stepney Tramways B 70 7
Allhallows - Branch Line to A 62 2
Alton - Branch Lines to A 11 8
Andover to Southampton A 82 7
Ascot - Branch Lines around A 64 9
Ashburton - Branch Line to B 95 2
Ashford - Steam to Eurostar B 67 7
Ashford to Dover A 48 7
Austrian Narrow Gauge D 04 7
Avonmouth - BL around D 42 X
B
Banbury to Birmingham D 27 6
Barking to Southend C 80 X
Barnet & Finchley Tramways B 93 6
Barry - Branch Lines around D 50 0
Basingstoke to Salisbury A 89 4
Bath Green Park to Bristol C 36 2
Bath to Evercreech Junction A 60 6
Bath Tramways B 86 3
Battle over Portsmouth 1940 A 29 0
Battle over Sussex 1940 A 79 7
Bedford to Wellingborough D 31 4
Betwixt Petersfield & Midhurst A 94 0
Blitz over Sussex 1941-42 B 35 9
Bodmin - Branch Lines around B 83 9
Bognor at War 1939-45 B 59 6
Bombers over Sussex 1943-45 B 51 0
Bournemouth & Poole Trys B 47 2
Bournemouth to Evercreech Jn A 46 0
Bournemouth to Weymouth A 57 6
Bournemouth Trolleybuses C 10 9
Bradford Trolleybuses D 19 5
Brecon to Neath D 43 8
Brecon to Newport D 16 0
Brickmaking in Sussex B 19 7
Brightons Tramways B 02 2 OOP
Brighton to Eastbourne A 16 9
Brighton to Worthing A 03 7
Brighton Trolleybuses D 34 9
Bristols Tramways B 57 X
Bristol to Taunton D 03 9
Bromley South to Rochester B 23 5
Bromsgrove to Gloucester D 73 X
Brunel - A railtour of his achievements D 74 8
Bude - Branch Line to B 29 4
Burnham to Evercreech Jn A 68 1
Burton & Ashby Tramways C 51 6
C
Camberwell & West Norwood Tys B 22 7
Cambridge to Ely D 55 1
Canterbury - Branch Lines around B 58 8
Cardiff Trolleybuses D 64 0
Caterham & Tattenham Corner B 25 1
Changing Midhurst C 15 X
Chard and Yeovil - BLs around C 30 3
Charing Cross to Dartford A 75 4
Charing Cross to Orpington A 96 7
Cheddar - Branch Line to B 90 1
Cheltenham to Andover C 43 5
Chesterfield Tramways D 37 3
Chesterfield Trolleybuses D 51 9
Chichester to Portsmouth A 14 2
Clapham & Streatham Trys B 97 9 OOP
Clapham Junction - 50 yrs C 06 0 OOP
Clapham Junction to Beckenham Jn B 36 7
Clevedon & Portishead - BLs to D 18 7
Collectors Trains, Trolleys & Trams D 29 2
Colonel Stephens D62 4
Cornwall Narrow Gauge D 56 X
Crawley to Littlehampton A 34 7
Cromer - Branch Lines around C 26 5
Croydons Tramways B 42 1
Croydons Trolleybuses B 73 1 OOP
Croydon to East Grinstead B 48 0
Crystal Palace (HL) & Catford Loop A 87 8
D
Darlington Trolleybuses D 33 0
Dartford to Sittingbourne B 34 0
Derby Tramways D 17 9
Derby Trolleybuses C 72 9
Derwent Valley - Branch Line to the D 06 3
Didcot to Banbury D 02 0
Didcot to Swindon C 84 2
Didcot to Winchester C 13 3
Dorset & Somerset Narrow Gauge D 76 4
Douglas to Peel C 88 5
Douglas to Port Erin C 55 9
Douglas to Ramsey D 39 X
Dovers Tramways B 24 3
Dover to Ramsgate A 78 9
E
Ealing to Slough C 42 7
Eastbourne to Hastings A 27 4
East Cornwall Mineral Railways D 22 5
East Croydon to Three Bridges A 53 3
East Grinstead - Branch Lines to A 07 X
East Ham & West Ham Tramways B 52 9
East Kent Light Railway A 61 4 OOP
East London - Branch Lines of C 44 3
East London Line B 80 4
East Ridings Secret Resistance D 21 7
Edgware & Willesden Tramways C 18 4
Effingham Junction - BLs around A 74 6
Eltham & Woolwich Tramways B 74 X OOP
Ely to Kings Lynn C 53 2
Ely to Norwich C 90 7
Embankment & Waterloo Tramways B 41 3
Enfield & Wood Green Trys C 03 6 OOP
Enfield Town & Palace Gates - BL to D 32 2
Epsom to Horsham A 30 4
Euston to Harrow & Wealdstone C 89 3
Exeter & Taunton Tramways B 32 4
Exeter to Barnstaple B 15 4
Exeter to Newton Abbot C 49 4
Exeter to Tavistock B 69 3
Exmouth - Branch Lines to B 00 6
F
Fairford - Branch Line to A 52 5
Falmouth, Helston & St. Ives - BL to C 74 5
Fareham to Salisbury A 67 3
Faversham to Dover B 05 7
Felixstowe & Aldeburgh - BL to D 20 9
Fenchurch Street to Barking C 20 6
Festiniog - 50 yrs of enterprise C 83 4
Festiniog in the Fifties B 68 5
Festiniog in the Sixties B 91 X
Finsbury Park to Alexandra Palace C 02 8
Frome to Bristol B 77 4
Fulwell - Trams, Trolleys & Buses D 11 X
G
Gloucester to Bristol D 35 7
Gloucester to Cardiff D 66 7
Gosport & Horndean Trys B 92 8
Gosport - Branch Lines around A 36 3
Great Yarmouth Tramways D 13 6
Greece Narrow Gauge D 72 1
Greenwich & Dartford Tramways B 14 6 OOP
Guildford to Redhill A 63 0
H
Hammersmith & Hounslow Trys C 33 8
Hampshire Narrow Gauge D 36 5
Hampshire Waterways A 84 3 OOP
Hampstead & Highgate Tramways B 53 7
Harrow to Watford D 14 4
Hastings to Ashford A 37 1 OOP
Hastings Tramways B 18 9
Hastings Trolleybuses B 81 2 OOP
Hawkhurst - Branch Line to A 66 5
Hayling - Branch Line to A 12 6
Haywards Heath to Seaford A 28 2
Henley, Windsor & Marlow - BL to C77 X
Hereford to Newport D 54 3
Hexham to CarlisleD 75 6
Hitchin to Peterborough D 07 1
Holborn & Finsbury Tramways B 79 0
Holborn Viaduct to Lewisham A 81 9
Horsham - Branch Lines to A 02 9
Huddersfield Trolleybuses C 92 3
Hull Tramways D60 8
Hull Trolleybuses D 24 1
Huntingdon - Branch Lines around A 93 2
I
Ilford & Barking Tramways B 61 8
Ilford to Shenfield C 97 4
Ilfracombe - Branch Line to B 21 9
Ilkeston & Glossop Tramways D 40 3
Industrial Rlys of the South East A 09 6
Ipswich to Saxmundham C 41 9
Ipswich Trolleybuses D 59 4
Isle of Wight Lines - 50 yrs C 12 5
K
Kent & East Sussex Waterways A 72 X
Kent Narrow Gauge C 45 1
Kent Seaways - Hoys to Hovercraft D 79 9
Kingsbridge - Branch Line to C 98 2
Kingston & Hounslow Loops A 83 5 OOP
Kingston & Wimbledon Tramways B 56 1
Kingswear - Branch Line to C 17 6
L
Lambourn - Branch Line to C 70 2
Launceston & Princetown - BL to C 19 2
Lewisham & Catford Tramways B 26 X OOP
Lewisham to Dartford A 92 4
Lines around Wimbledon B 75 8
Liverpool Street to Chingford D 01 2
Liverpool Street to Ilford C 34 6
Liverpool Tramways - Eastern C 04 4
Liverpool Tramways - Northern C 46 X
Liverpool Tramways - Southern C 23 0
London Bridge to Addiscombe B 20 0
London Bridge to East Croydon A 58 4
London Chatham & Dover Railway A 88 6
London Termini - Past and Proposed D 00 4
London to Portsmouth Waterways B 43 X
Longmoor - Branch Lines to A 41 X
Looe - Branch Line to C 22 2
Lyme Regis - Branch Line to A 45 2
Lynton - Branch Line to B 04 9
M
Maidstone & Chatham Tramways B 40 5
Maidstone Trolleybuses C 00 1 OOP
March - Branch Lines around B 09 X
Margate & Ramsgate Tramways C 52 4
Marylebone to Rickmansworth D49 7
Midhurst - Branch Lines around A 49 5
Midhurst - Branch Lines to A 01 0 OOP
Military Defence of West Sussex A 23 1
Military Signals, South Coast C 54 0
Minehead - Branch Line to A 80 0
Mitcham Junction Lines B 01 4
Mitchell & company C 59 1
Monmouthshire Eastern Valleys D 71 3
Moreton-in-Marsh to Worcester D 26 8
Moretonhampstead - BL to C 27 3
N
Newbury to Westbury C 66 4
Newcastle to Hexham D 69 1
Newcastle Trolleybuses D 78 0
Newport (IOW) - Branch Lines to A 26 6
Newquay - Branch Lines to C 71 0
Newton Abbot to Plymouth C 60 5
Northern France Narrow Gauge C 75 3
North East German Narrow Gauge D 44 6
North Kent Tramways B 44 8
North London Line B 94 4
North Woolwich - BLs around C 65 6
Norwich Tramways C 40 0
Nottinghamshire & Derbyshire T/B D 63 2
Nottinghamshire & Derbyshire T/W D 53 5
O
Orpington to Tonbridge B 03 0 OOP
Oxford to Bletchley D57 8
Oxford to Moreton-in-Marsh D 15 2
P
Paddington to Ealing C 37 0
Paddington to Princes Risborough C 81 8
Padstow - Branch Line to B 54 5
Plymouth - BLs around B 98 7
Plymouth to St. Austell C 63 X
Pontypool to Mountain Ash D 65 9
Porthmadog 1954-94 - BL around B 31 6
Porthmadog to Blaenau B 50 2 OOP
Portmadoc 1923-46 - BL around B 13 8
Portsmouths Tramways B 72 3
Portsmouth to Southampton A 31 2
Portsmouth Trolleybuses C 73 7
Potters Bar to Cambridge D 70 5
Princes Risborough - Branch Lines to D 05 5
Princes Risborough to Banbury C 85 0
R
Railways to Victory C 16 8/7 OOP
Reading to Basingstoke B 27 8
Reading to Didcot C 79 6
Reading to Guildford A 47 9 OOP
Reading Tramways B 87 1
Reading Trolleybuses C 05 2
Redhill to Ashford A 73 8
Return to Blaenau 1970-82 C 64 8
Rickmansworth to Aylesbury D 61 6
Roman Roads of Hampshire D 67 5
Roman Roads of Surrey C 61 3
Roman Roads of Sussex C 48 6
Romneyrail C 32 X
Ryde to Ventnor A 19 3
S
Salisbury to Westbury B 39 1
Salisbury to Yeovil B 06 5 OOP
Saxmundham to Yarmouth C 69 9
Saxony Narrow Gauge D 47 0
Seaton & Eastbourne Tramways B 76 6 OOP
Seaton & Sidmouth - Branch Lines to A 95 9
Secret Sussex Resistance B 82 0
SECR Centenary album C 11 7
Selsey - Branch Line to A 04 5
Sheerness - Branch Lines around B 16 2
Shepherds Bush to Uxbridge T/Ws C 28 1
Shrewsbury - Branch Line to A 86 X
Sierra Leone Narrow Gauge D 28 4
Sittingbourne to Ramsgate A 90 8
Slough to Newbury C 56 7
Solent - Creeks, Crafts & Cargoes D 52 7
Southamptons Tramways B 33 2
Southampton to Bournemouth A 42 8
Southend-on-Sea Tramways B 28 6
Southern France Narrow Gauge C 47 8
Southwark & Deptford Tramways B 38 3
Southwold - Branch Line to A 15 0
South Eastern & Chatham Railways C 08 7
South London Line B 46 4
South London Tramways 1903-33 D 10 1
St. Albans to Bedford D 08 X
St. Austell to Penzance C 67 2
St. Pancras to Barking D 68 3
St. Pancras to St. Albans C 78 8
Stamford Hill Tramways B 85 5
Steaming through Cornwall B 30 8 OOP
Steaming through Kent A 13 4 OOP
Steaming through the Isle of Wight A 56 8
Steaming through West Hants A 69 X
Stratford upon avon to Birmingham D 772
Stratford upon Avon to Cheltenham C 25 7
Strood to Paddock Wood B 12 X
Surrey Home Guard C 57 5
Surrey Narrow Gauge C 87 7
Surrey Waterways A 51 7 OOP
Sussex Home Guard C 24 9
Sussex Narrow Gauge C 68 0
Sussex Shipping Sail, Steam & Motor D 23 3
Swanley to Ashford B 45 6
Swindon to Bristol C 96 6
Swindon to Gloucester D46 2
Swindon to Newport D 30 6
Swiss Narrow Gauge C 94 X
T
Talyllyn - 50 years C 39 7
Taunton to Barnstaple B 60 X
Taunton to Exeter C 82 6
Tavistock to Plymouth B 88 X
Tees-side Trolleybuses D 58 6
Tenterden - Branch Line to A 21 5
Thanet's Tramways B 11 1 OOP
Three Bridges to Brighton A 35 5
Tilbury Loop C 86 9
Tiverton - Branch Lines around C 62 1
Tivetshall to Beccles D 41 1
Tonbridge to Hastings A 44 4
Torrington - Branch Lines to B 37 5
Tunbridge Wells - Branch Lines to A 32 0
Twickenham & Kingston Trys C 35 4
Two-Foot Gauge Survivors C 21 4 OOP
U
Upwell - Branch Line to B 64 2
V
Victoria & Lambeth Tramways B 49 9
Victoria to Bromley South A 98 3
Victoria to East Croydon A 40 1 OOP
Vivarais C 31 1
W
Walthamstow & Leyton Tramways B 65 0
Waltham Cross & Edmonton Trys C 07 9
Wandsworth & Battersea Tramways B 63 4
Wantage - Branch Line to D 25 X
Wareham to Swanage - 50 yrs D 09 8
War on the Line A 10 X
War on the Line VIDEO + 88 0
Waterloo to Windsor A 54 1
Waterloo to Woking A 38 X
Watford to Leighton Buzzard D 45 4
Wenford Bridge to Fowey C 09 5
Westbury to Bath B 55 3
Westbury to Taunton C 76 1
West Cornwall Mineral Railways D 48 9
West Croydon to Epsom B 08 1
West London - Branch Lines of C 50 8
West London Line B 84 7
West Sussex Waterways A 24 X OOP
West Wiltshire - Branch Lines of D 12 8
Weymouth - Branch Lines around A 65 7
Willesden Junction to Richmond B 71 5
Wimbledon to Beckenham C 58 3
Wimbledon to Epsom B 62 6
Wimborne - Branch Lines around A 97 5
Wisbech - Branch Lines around C 01 X
Wisbech 1800-1901 C 93 1
Woking to Alton A 59 2
Woking to Portsmouth A 25 8
Woking to Southampton A 55 X
Woolwich & Dartford Trolleys B 66 9 OOP
Worcester to Hereford D 38 1
Worthing to Chichester A 06 1
Y
Yeovil - 50 yrs change C 38 9
Yeovil to Dorchester A 76 2 OOP
Yeovil to Exeter A 91 6